A. D. Hope

Twayne's English Authors Series

Kinley Roby, Editor

TEAS 539

A. D. HOPE
Photograph by Loui Seslja, NLA Photographics, 1991. By permission of the National Library of Australia.

A. D. Hope

Robert Darling

Keuka College

Twayne Publishers
An Imprint of Simon & Schuster Macmillan
New York

Prentice Hall International
London • Mexico City • New Delhi • Singapore • Sydney • Toronto

Twayne's English Authors Series No. 539

A. D. Hope
Robert Darling

Copyright © 1997 by Twayne Publishers

Twayne Publishers
An Imprint of Simon & Schuster Macmillan
1633 Broadway
New York, NY 10019

Library of Congress Cataloging-in-Publication Data

Darling, Robert.
    A. D. Hope / Robert Darling.
        p.   cm.— (Twayne's English authors series ; TEAS 539)
    Includes bibliographical references and index.
    ISBN 0–8057–7049–6
    1. Hope, A. D. (Alec Derwent), 1907–   —Criticism and
interpretation.   2. Australia—In literature.   I. Title.
II Series.
PR9619.3.H65Z58   1997
821—dc21   96–48186
                                                    CIP

The paper used in this publication meets the minimum requirements of American National Standard for Information Sciences—Permanence of Paper for Printed Library Materials. ANSI Z39.48–1984. ∞ ™

10 9 8 7 6 5 4 3 2

Printed in the United States of America

Contents

Preface

This study explores the poetic achievement of the Australian poet A. D. Hope by tracing the major thematic trends of his verse. The excellence of his lifetime's work has gone unjustifiably ignored in the United States, and thus this book is intended as both an appraisal and an appreciation.

Hope's life has spanned most of the twentieth century, a century whose prevailing tastes were often not to Hope's liking. He has suffered a critical neglect in this country as a result of his defiance of the major trends of modernism and postmodernism; from the first, he has cast himself as an outsider. But at this particularly fractious point in our literary tradition, there are several younger poets and critics who are claiming Hope as something of a father figure; indeed, several of the themes sounded by some in poetry today—a return to narrative, the use of the discursive mode, the importance of traditional form, the necessity that poetry communicate beyond the inner circle of the initiate—were far earlier given voice in Hope's criticism and in his practice of poetry.

Because Australian poetry is even less known to the American reader than is Hope, I next consider the general tradition of poetry in Australia. Although I contend that poetry in the English language has much in common despite national differences, still I must concede that regional variations are important and need to be considered. Next I address the vexed question of Hope's Australianism; he is often thought to be more of an internationalist than a noticeably Australian poet. However, his work is influenced greatly, though at times quite subtly so, by his native land. Those who don't recognize the important Australian element in Hope's work are perhaps too busy searching for kangaroos.

His satire, a relatively minor aspect of his work but the one for which he is best known in America, is considered next. Satire has been a neglected genre in this century and Hope attempts to revive it. He is only partially successful, though; too often the necessarily light touch of the satirist becomes weighed down with the heavy hand of invective. While Hope has written some memorable satire, it is not his major mode.

I next concern myself with an analysis of Hope's poems of physical disgust and failed love. For a poet long known for his celebration of

erotic love, Hope's work, especially in midcareer, maintains an element of disgust with the physical world, a sense of death inherent in the act of creation. Although these poems—and there are several of them—do not constitute Hope's final word on the subject, they include some of his strongest poems. Those that fail do so by coming too close to nihilism and misogyny.

Next, I focus on Hope's use of the heroic mode. Hope is very much a poet of dualities; he needs to work with antinomies to create a tension that can lead to transcendence. But the heroic mode was inadequate to his needs—being, in a sense, the worst of romantic gestures. Hope came to reshape or reframe the heroic into the mythic, which better fits the demands of his poetry. The speech of the warrior gave way to the speech of the gods.

The mythic, which is termed the night vision, is then placed beside the vision of the day, the scientific. The tension resultant from this duality makes possible a sense of the transcendent, that which supersedes dualities and at the same time confirms them. Hope, despite his strong civic impulses, is at heart a vatic poet. From the beginning of his career, poetry has been a substitute religion for Hope; it is his intimation of a truer world.

This study concludes with an appraisal of Hope's standing in relation to the other poets of this century. The ending thus attempts to reunite the entire corpus of Hope's work, which is necessarily fragmented by a thematic study. Hope's range is very wide, as time after time he explores the grand themes so many of his contemporaries shun.

I have written this book as an introduction to Hope's work, an opus large enough to require many volumes of criticism. He is an interesting and opinionated critic, but I shall consider his criticism only as it illuminates his poetry, which is where his greatness lies. I seek to show Hope's major concerns, problems he has dealt with over decades. The disadvantage of such an approach is that certain strong poems that are atypical of Hope in their themes are not extensively considered, but I think this shortcoming insignificant to my purpose of introducing the perceptive reader to the major themes of an important body of work.

Acknowledgments

Parts of chapter 6 were revised from my chapter on A. D. Hope published in *International Literature in English,* edited by Robert Ross and published by Garland in 1991. I would also like to thank series editor Kinley Roby; Nancy Potter, Paul Petrie, and Wallace Sillanpoa who read this manuscript in its early stages; and Dana Gioia who offered some kindly encouragement when it was most needed.

Chronology

1907   Alec Derwent Hope born in Cooma, New South Wales, 21 July, the first of five children of Percival and Flo Hope.

1911   Family moves to Tasmania.

1918   Hope sent to Leslie House, a Quaker school, in Hobart.

1921   Family moves back to New South Wales. Hope registered at Bathurst High School.

1924   Graduates from Fort Street Boy's High School.

1928   Graduates in English and Philosophy from the University of Sydney. Wins scholarship to University College, Oxford.

1931   Graduates from Oxford with a third-class degree.

1932   Returns to Sydney. Trains at Sydney Teachers' College. Becomes resident tutor at St. Paul's College.

1934   Becomes vocational psychologist for the Department of Labour and Industry.

1936   Educational research for the Department of Education. Becomes engaged.

1937   Marries Penelope Robinson. Appointed lecturer in education at Sydney Teachers' College.

1938   Appointed lecturer in English at Sydney Teachers' College.

1940   Daughter, Emily, born.

1944   Twin sons, Andrew and Gregory, born.

1945   Appointed senior lecturer in English at the University of Melbourne.

1951   Appointed professor of English at Canberra University College (now the Australian National University).

1955   *The Wandering Islands*. Wins Grace Leven Prize.

1960   *Poems*.

1963   *Selected Poems. Australian Literature 1950–1962.*

1964   President of the Australian Association for the Teaching of English.

1965   *The Cave and the Spring. Collected Poems 1930–1965.* Wins Australian Arts Award.

1966   Wins R. A. Crouch Memorial Award.

1967   Retires from teaching. Elected professor emeritus. Wins Sydney Myer Charity Trust Award.

1969   *New Poems 1965–69.* Wins Levinson Prize for Poetry and the Ingram Merrill Award for Literature. Appointed Library Fellow at the Australian National University and special consultant in poetry at the Library of Congress in Washington, D.C.

1970   *A Midsummer Eve's Dream* and *Dunciad Minor.*

1972   *Collected Poems.* Given the Order of the British Empire.

1974   *Native Companions.*

1975   *Judith Wright* and *A Late Picking.*

1976   Wins Robert Frost Award for Poetry and the *Age* Book Award.

1978   *A Book of Answers* and *The Pack of Autolycus.*

1979   *The New Cratylus.* Daughter dies.

1981   *Antechinus.* Made Companion of the Order of Australia.

1982   *Doctor Faustus.*

1983   *Tre Volti Dell' Amore.*

1985   *The Age of Reason.* Appointed Ashby Visiting Fellow, Clare Hall College, Cambridge, and Honorary Fellow of University College, Oxford.

1987   *Ladies from the Sea.*

1988   Wife dies.

1991   *Orpheus.*

1992   *Chance Encounters.*

Introduction

Although A. D. Hope is Australia's most widely honored poet, his name is not well known outside his native country and his work is even less familiar than his name. The only collection of Hope's poetry currently in print in the United States is from Carcanet, a British publisher; no American editions have been published since Viking brought out its third volume of his verse in 1970, despite the fact that his work has consistently received favorable notice from American reviewers.

Hope is very much an institution in Australia, though even in his native land a surprisingly large number of his books are out of print. This may be the result of his having become such an institution that he is in danger of being taken for granted. The English department at the Australian National University in Canberra is housed in the A. D. Hope Building, and Hope has received most accolades available to an English-language poet. Longevity is not an unalloyed blessing in contemporary literary culture, which is always thirsting for the new. Yet Hope is probably the central figure in the coming of age of Australian poetry and is an important poet internationally for the English-speaking community.

Alec Derwent Hope was born in Cooma, New South Wales, on 21 July 1907, the first of five children of Percival and Flo Hope, he a Presbyterian minister and she a teacher before her marriage. In 1911, the Hopes moved to Campbell Town in the Macquaise Valley on the island of Tasmania. In his early years, Hope was educated at home, in most disciplines by his mother and in Latin by his father. His parents owned an extensive library in classical, English, and religious literature but lacked a single volume of Australian creative writing; such a neglect of what was viewed as too provincial a literature for educated tastes was not unusual in early twentieth-century Australia. Habits from the old country were often adhered to rigidly. Indeed, most of the houses in Tasmania were built facing the south, as is the Scottish and English fashion, despite the fact that in the southern hemisphere this meant that the backs of the houses received the most sunshine.

The low income for country pastors was supplemented by the minister being graced not only with a manse but also with a farm that was worked by parishioners. The local schoolroom was a sheep-shearing shed

and was too far away for Hope to attend with any regularity, except during sheep-shearing time when class was held on his father's farm.

Hope has written poetry for as long as he can remember, but the first
specific effort he can call to mind was a "pious rhyme in fifty-two stanzas—one for each week in the year—composed for my mother's birth-
day and designed to encourage her in her Christian duty." Hope was
about eight at this time and remembers that his mother "gently suggested that I might perhaps consider improving my own conduct rather
than hers."[1]

For more formal schooling, Hope was sent in 1918 to Leslie House, a
Quaker school in Hobart. In 1921, Hope's family moved back to New
South Wales, and Hope was sent ahead of them so his move would not
conflict with the school year. Hope was registered at Bathurst High
School, and it was during this time that he became infatuated with a
young painter named Violet McKee. She took the teenager on as something of a protégé, despite the fact that Hope was not pursuing a calling
in the visual arts. Hope remembers that he was "busy turning out second-hand Swinburne verse of intense passion and probably appalling
imitation of his diction."[2] McKee had the aspiring poet bring her his
work and commented that he should burn them and begin to write
from his own experience, from things that he knew best. Hope duly
built his *auto-da-fé* and considers this advice one of only two poetry
lessons he had in his life.

After leaving Bathurst, Hope repeated his last year of secondary education at Fort Street Boy's High School in Sydney to qualify for a scholarship to college, a necessity considering how poorly ministers such as
his father were paid. Hope was then admitted to the University of Sydney where he wanted to study medicine; however, because of his academic background and talents, he ended up reading English and philosophy, the latter of which at that time included psychology. He was also
coeditor of the university *Arts Journal*.

Hope graduated from Sydney in 1928 with a University Medal in
philosophy and won a scholarship to University College, Oxford, to read
English. Oxford's discipline at that time consisted primarily of philolog-
ical studies, for which Hope was woefully underprepared. Hope also
panicked during his exams and left in 1931 with a third-class degree,
which is the lowest one can receive and still graduate. Many years later
he remarked "I am still in disgrace with myself" (*CE*, 74).

But Hope's English experience was important to him in other ways
than his failure as a linguist. (Given the immense range of languages the

poet has learned over his lifetime, however, it is hard to think of him as having failed.) Although he just missed Auden and the group of students gathered around him, Hope studied under such notable faculty members as C. L. Wrenn, J. R. R. Tolkien, and C. S. Lewis. Wrenn and Lewis adopted contrasting techniques with the young Australian; Hope remarked that Lewis "educated me by ignoring me as Wrenn did by patient and devoted teaching" (*CE,* 67). Hope was shocked at the rigid class structure he found in the society—far more stratified than in Australia—but also experienced the living tradition of the West that had been real for him to that point only in his reading. In particular, his vacations spent at Lacock Abbey in Wiltshire, now owned by the National Trust, afforded him an intimate sense of the living tradition: "I was keenly aware that the room I was working in contained other and unseen persons, friendly and genial" (*CE,* 71).

This was not the spirit he encountered when he returned to Sydney in 1931. His low mood about his degree was not eased when he tried to discover how to survive with the economic depression in full force. He could find no lasting employment and was such a dark cloud around the house that his father sent him off to camp on land he owned in the country. It was there that Hope began to teach himself Russian and to emend the text of Marlowe's *Doctor Faustus,* a task he would not complete for nearly half a century.

Returning to Sydney in 1932, Hope trained at Sydney Teachers' College—quite a change from the heady atmosphere of Oxford—and became a resident tutor in arts at St. Paul's College. He hated the teaching and discipline but took full advantage of Sydney's Bohemian night life. This Jekyll-and-Hyde existence must have seemed even more extreme in 1933 when he became a relief teacher in Sydney secondary schools.

In 1934 Hope became a vocational psychologist for the Department of Labour and Industry. Hope considered his two years at this position mainly an example of bureaucratic waste, and in 1936 he began some educational research for the Department of Education and moved temporarily to Canberra to take charge of a trades school there. During this time he met Penelope Robinson. By the time Hope returned to Sydney in late 1936 he was engaged.

In 1937 Hope was appointed a lecturer in education at Sydney Teachers' College. This employment allowed him to marry Penelope but otherwise was another example of a job for which Hope was ill suited. For his first course, Hope "bought the textbook and managed to keep a

chapter or so ahead of the class" (CE, 87). While this is not a unique incident in academics, Hope's next class was every teacher's nightmare. Hope knew nothing about statistics and discovered that there were several honor students in his class who were far better acquainted with the material than their fumbling teacher. These students ended up teaching the class with Hope on the sidelines attempting to learn.

Hope also had lessons of another sort from one of the members of the class. James McAuley was a promising young poet among the students and read through Hope's poems, telling him which should be kept and which discarded. This was Hope's second and last instruction in poetry; McAuley's tastes had matured faster than Hope's. This time cemented a friendship that was to last the rest of McAuley's life, before his premature death robbed Australia of one of its best poets.

Fortunately, in 1938 Hope was appointed a lecturer in English at Sydney Teachers' College. Hope remarks that he "moved thankfully into it and tried to forget that I ever called myself a psychologist" (CE, 89). A more secure position was accompanied by parenthood—a daughter, Emily, was born in 1940, and twin sons, Andrew and Gregory, in 1944.

During these years Hope had yet to publish any books, although a few of his poems had reached print, but he possessed a growing reputation as a caustic critic of the Australian literary scene. He was harsh in his criticism of the Jindyworobak movement, which tried to create an Australian literature by stocking lines full of references to indigenous Australian objects and rejecting the language's English tradition. Hope was equally dismissive of a group of pseudomodernists, who were led by Max Harris and published a magazine, Angry Penguins, which represented the worst tendencies of the modernist movement. James McAuley and fellow poet Harold Stewart submitted intentionally poor poems written by a poet they invented, Ern Malley, whom Angry Penguins published and hailed as the modernist poet who would put Australia on the literary map. When the hoax was first exposed, Hope was considered the prime suspect; indeed, he was aware of the plot. Though Hope is also a critic who can praise, his attacks on Patrick White and other writers have left him enemies to this day. On a less controversial note, at this time Hope was also the radio personality Anthony Inkwell who conducted poetry programs for children on the Australian Broadcasting System.

With increasing recognition, in 1945 Hope was appointed a senior lecturer in the department of English at the University of Melbourne. He served in this capacity until he accepted the post of professor of Eng-

lish at Canberra University College in 1951. Although his title was an advancement, Canberra UC was a satellite of Melbourne. However, a few years after Hope moved, the school gained its independence as the Australian National University.

When he first came to Canberra, Hope instituted a course in Australian literature, the first formal university course offered in the country's English language literature. Melbourne refused to give credit for the course. Critics who fault him for his supposed lack of identification with Antipodean culture conveniently overlook Hope's pioneering efforts to establish the academic respectability of Australian work.

When Hope was changing houses in Canberra, he stored most of his manuscripts at the school so they would not be lost. As fate would have it, that wing of the school burned and almost all of Hope's work was destroyed. What remained was the manuscript of what was to be his first book, *The Wandering Islands*. Thus we have almost nothing of Hope's early work. Interestingly, an event such as this is often more of a disaster for the critic than for the poet.

Hope had some difficulty getting his collection published, despite its having been awaited with considerable interest by the literary community. Melbourne University Press turned down the manuscript, probably out of concern for offending the censorship standards still draconian by modern standards in 1950s Australia. The book finally appeared in a handsome edition from Edwards & Shaw of Sydney; Hope had his first book published at the age of 48.

Hope was a deliberate worker, slow to mature as a poet, and active as a teacher and critic, but censorship was the major reason for such a late publication. Until the 1950s, Australia had a far more repressive obscenity law than did America. And Hope is a very sensual poet; love is his major theme, and physical love pervades his entire poetic canon. Cecil Hadgraft, in a survey of Australian literature, put his mathematical skills to use and discovered that of the 42 poems in *The Wandering Islands*, 24 contain sexual imagery, "fifteen of them having direct images," while the remaining nine have "indirect references to the relevant anatomy."[3] That a critic would spend time constructing a body count of sexual allusions is an indication of how pervasive the puritanical influence was in Australia.

Nevertheless, *The Wandering Islands* received much praise and won the Grace Leven Prize. The publication of Hope's first book unleashed a series of books and resultant awards. *Poems,* a selection of some of the poems in *The Wandering Islands* and in several uncollected pieces, was

published in both Australia and the United States in 1960. In Australia, Hope published his *Selected Poems* in the *Australian Poets Series,* which won an Arts Council Award in 1965, and a chapbook of critical commentary, *Australian Literature: 1950–1962.* With awards and an honored teaching position, Hope was able to travel widely at last and until his 80s was a frequent and observant tourist in most areas of the world, most often in Europe. He has held visiting professorships twice in the United States. Back in Australia, he was from 1964 to 1967 president of the Australian Association for the Teaching of English, quite a progress from the fumbling teacher of statistics three decades earlier.

Hope's first substantial publication of critical essays in book form was *The Cave and the Spring,* published in 1965, which won the Britannica Australia Award and the Volkswagen Award the following year. That same year saw the publication of *Collected Poems 1930–1965,* which won the Australian Arts Award, the R. A. Crouch Memorial Gold Medal, and the Sydney Myer Charity Trust Award. In 1967, Hope retired from teaching and was elected professor emeritus.

Since retirement, Hope's life has been one of publications, travel, and awards. His *New Poems 1965–1969* brought him the Levinson Prize for Poetry and the Ingram Merrill Award for Literature, as well as appointments as library fellow at the Australian National University and special consultant in poetry at the Library of Congress in Washington, D.C. Strangely, this collection is the last to be published by an American publisher.

That a poet who was rapidly, almost dizzyingly, becoming a widely known, internationally published poet after his fiftieth year should suddenly again become primarily published only in his native country is surprising, especially since his work did not decline noticeably in either value or volume. Part of the reason may be that Hope's conservative poetic practices and outspoken antimodernist critical views began to run even more seriously counter to the times. Hope is a compatible figure when judged with such poets as W. H. Auden, Richard Wilbur, Anthony Hecht, X. J. Kennedy, and others. But through the late 1950s and 1960s many poets who had worked in traditional forms abandoned them for free verse, or at least looser forms, and the Beat and Confessional movements, coupled with the chaos of the Vietnam War, made all received forms and values suspect. Academe, which is increasingly the refuge of poets and poetry publication, is usually about a decade behind, and by the late 1970s many positions in universities and at poetry publishers were held by a younger generation that had neither worked in

traditional forms nor really understood their value. Such a climate would not be conducive to an aging though active poet. Someone such as Wilbur would seem an anomaly; an Australian formalist could be dismissed as a neocolonial, still pining for the mother country, a marooned Brit.

The next year, 1970, brought another two books, *A Midsummer Eve's Dream,* a long, fascinating, but ultimately questionable explication of Scottish cultural sources behind William Dunbar's "The Tretis of the Tua Mariit Wemen and the Wedo," along with *Dunciad Minor,* a lengthy verse satire done in the manner of Pope's *Dunciad* and attacking contemporary literary criticism.

The deluge of publications and awards continued unabated. His *Collected Poems* of 1972 helped earn Hope an Order of the British Empire and his first of several honorary degrees. *Native Companions,* a collection of literary essays, many with autobiographical tendencies, followed in 1974, while 1975 was marked with a critical work on the Australian poet Judith Wright and a new poetry collection, *A Late Picking.*

Still the honors flowed in: in 1976 Hope received the Robert Frost Award for Poetry and the *Age* Book Award. Two years later Hope published *A Book of Answers,* a lighter collection in which he writes poems responding to poems by other poets, and *The Pack of Autolycus,* a collection of essays dealing with random topics of interest to Hope through eight centuries of literature. *The New Cratylus,* Hope's major statement on poetic practice, in which he remained unrepentant in his attack on twentieth-century poetics, was published in 1979.

But time moved on and brought loss. Loved colleagues such as Ian Maxwell and James McAuley died, and the year of the publication of *Cratylus* saw the death of Hope's daughter, Emily. Still, Hope relentlessly continued with his writing and publishing. His old age is one of the remarkable stories in poetry; at an advanced age when many poets cease writing Hope has been amazingly productive.

The year 1981 brought yet another poetry collection, *Antechinus,* and the awarding of a Companion of the Order of Australia, while the following year witnessed Hope's emendations to Marlowe's *Tragical History of Doctor Faustus,* completed 50 years after its beginning. More international, but non-American, recognition followed in 1983 with the translation of many of Hope's love poems into Italian in a volume entitled *Tre Volti Dell' Amore.* Hope had long preached the virtues of the discursive mode and narrative poetry, and when he was 78 published *The Age of Reason,* a collection of narrative poems dealing with subjects from the

eighteenth century. This same year, 1985, brought his appointment both as Ashby Visiting Fellow, Clare Hall, Cambridge, and as Honorary Fellow of University College, Oxford, from where he had left in disappointment five decades earlier.

At the age of 80, Hope published his first play, *Ladies from the Sea,* a lively imagining of Circe and Calypso coming to call on a chagrined Odysseus in Ithaca. While the play is good fun, it does not make one wish that Hope had devoted himself to drama rather than poetry.

In 1988, Hope's wife, Penelope, died. Still the poet continued. He published another poetry collection, *Orpheus,* in 1991, which, though uneven, contains a few of the best poems ever written by a poet in his ninth decade, and a loosely connected memoir, *Chance Encounters,* the following year. As of this writing, he is still at work on his own poetry and translations.

Hope's is a remarkable creative life, the relative public silence of its first half releasing a torrent of creation, publication, and honors in its second half. He is still underappreciated, especially in the United States. A. D. Hope should be recognized for his considerable achievement, an achievement that, ignored, would leave incomplete the record of twentieth-century poetry in English.

Chapter One
The Australian Tradition

The poetry of any nation is affected to some extent by the topography of the country in which it is written; indeed, it can be argued that a great deal of the national character is molded in reaction to landscape. When the geography of a country is imposing, not only in its beauty but also in its ferocity, or when a country is relatively new in that it does not have an established cultural tradition, then the attitudes of the poets toward the land they occupy become more and more decisive in the fostering of a literature. What merely lurks in the background in an established tradition becomes an essential part of the subject matter, entwined with thematic concerns, in the quest for a sense of national identity.

The English conquest of Australia is relatively recent; additionally, the country has a landscape and a climate that were uncongenial to early settlement. Even if Australia had not been established as a penal colony, it would not have drawn immigrants as the United States did. In addition to its climate, its utter remoteness made it seem almost another planet. Before more modern means of transportation, relocation to Australia required a journey that could consume the better part of the year, with no real assurance of safe transport. There still remain to this day vast tracts of the continent that are virtually uninhabitable.

Any colonial culture is torn between the particular facts of the immediate environment and the sustaining tradition of the mother country. A tradition gives the uprooted settler a sense of identity, yet can also seem very much out of place in the new locale. Settlers find they have been changed and discover old ways already becoming foreign to them. Yet the new can seem unfathomably strange as well. In Australia, this natural tension was exaggerated because of the country's isolation, its recent status as a colony, the utter foreignness of its aspect to the English invader, and its immensity. It is the only country in the world that is also a continent.

From the beginning, white Australians have taken two different approaches regarding their country. One is to embrace its newness and proclaim their independence from the traditions of the old country. The American example is perhaps indicative of this approach. The credo of

the new, rejection of English ways, and taking the land by force all found expression in nineteenth-century America. It is something of an imperialistic attitude toward one's own soil. The other at its most extreme is an attempt to maintain their customs as if the old country had never been left. Certainly the Canadian attitude has often bordered on this stance. Ties to the mother country are often assiduously maintained, and there is a sense of the land as something more to be survived than to be conquered. Australian writers have wavered between these two alternatives.

The former position was voiced most militantly in Australian literature by a group in the 1930s and 1940s called the Jindyworobaks, whose founder, Rex Ingamells, briefly stated their position in *Conditional Culture:* "The real test of a people's culture is the way in which they can express themselves in relation to their environment, and the loftiness and universality of their artistic conceptions raised on that basis. . . . It has been a piteous custom to write of Australian things with the English idiom, an idiom which can achieve exactness in England but not here."[1]

Such a position is certainly defensible insofar as one can use the particulars of one's situation to invoke universal truths; the Irish poet Patrick Kavanaugh once claimed all epics began in a local quarrel. But the Jindyworobaks searched too hard for novelty; in invoking the Australian scene, they became merely provincial—their exploitation of the particulars of their country separated them from the mainstream not only of poetry in English but from that of developing Australia as well. In the modern world, most developing countries tend to become more similar, their national peculiarities becoming more submerged by the internationalizing tendencies of communication and trade, both commercial and intellectual. Whether through overzealousness, dogmatism, or simple lack of talent, the Jindyworobaks became merely a curiosity, even in Australia.

Another problem with the Jindyworobaks' approach, and indeed with any self-consciously indigenous effort in the English-speaking world, is the exact meaning of the "English idiom." It is quite possible that Ingamells *et al.* meant traditional metrics (their own work indicates that English prosody was one of the major elements they rejected), but it is hard to see how iambic pentameter is particularly unsuited to the Australian sun. Many of the Jindyworobaks in their time and many poets of the past two decades have dropped traditional scansion, but in so doing have not produced anything that could be labeled a particularly Australian idiom; rather, their work appears curiously American in

that it seems most influenced by William Carlos Williams and his followers.

Certainly, many nouns were different in Jindyworobak poems: the vegetation and wildlife of England and Australia are worlds apart. But writing "kangaroo" instead of "deer" does not create a new idiom. If the Jindyworobaks believed that a Wordsworthian approach to nature is inappropriate in Australia, they were concerned with honesty of perception, not with the creation of an idiom.

Simply stated, poetry in English is English poetry, with regional variations. James McAuley distinguished between what he considered the provincialism of the Jindyworobaks and the healthy regionalism open to Australian poets. For McAuley, a healthy regionalism demanded a cultural tradition that would in turn produce works that would draw on traditional forms: "Where there is a strong central intellectual tradition one may expect to find the artistic conventions in a healthy state: a high degree of formality which has not stiffened into inflexibility."[2]

To use an American analogy, whereas the Jindyworobaks were the cowboys, McAuley was the Easterner who was bent on bringing civilization to the range. McAuley found it to Australia's disadvantage that its arts began to come of age just at the advent of modernism, a movement that called into question all formalities. The literary tenets and traditions that would guide poets in this new cultural wilderness of Australia were themselves being challenged. McAuley also anticipates an objection that his beliefs are aristocratic and therefore antipathetic to Australian sentiment: "I do not believe that the price of democracy is necessarily semi-barbarism" (McAuley 1985, 216).

Though most Australian poets can be found to occupy a middle ground somewhere between these two extremes, almost all from the beginning have had a preoccupation with their land, a preoccupation that still exists, as a glance at any anthology of Australian verse will verify. What struck the white invader first was the utter strangeness of the land. The European settlers found a land where the seasons were reversed, where the night sky was totally unfamiliar, where swans were black and foxes flew, where grass grew on trees that kept their leaves and shed their bark, where forests regenerated themselves by burning down, and where the only human inhabitants were among the most primitive peoples on Earth. Of course, the aborigines were treated as if they were not human at all and were slaughtered by the thousands. And everywhere was the bush, the outback, seeming to stretch on forever, unknowable and spiritually impenetrable.

Patrick White's novel *Voss* is very much a desert *Heart of Darkness,* the European meeting a darkness and finding the horror of his own being as easily in the outback as in the Belgian Congo. The bush influences how even the most innocent objects were perceived; the poet Eve Langley notes that even "Springtime at the core" appears as "a small child lost in the bush for ever more."[3] Evident in much Australian poetry of this century is a feeling of the utter otherness of Australia, a reaction that has vacillated somewhere between uneasiness and horror at this alien nature of the scene. R. A. Simpson wrote in "Landscape" that the "river is a thought that pours slowly / Down from nowhere" and claims that the "landscape also has its moving fears." He compares this landscape to an alien intelligence that he "cannot tell just what it thinks or knows. . . ."[4]

Yet the landscape, for all its strangeness, begins to take on human characteristics for many poets. In "South Country," Kenneth Slessor presents the land in its "whey-faced anonymity," its "flat earth of empty farms" as a "monstrous continent" of "rotting sunlight and the black, / Bruised flesh of thunderstorms." Yet in this image of horror there is something both human and inhuman wherein the "dwindled hills" appear as if "Something below pushed up a knob of skull, / Feeling its way to air."[5] The landscape takes on human qualities, but does so in a way that makes them seem a brutal parody; the viewer begins to discover this savage, uncivilized landscape has become a frightening part of the self. This emerging realization makes one see more clearly, sometimes too clearly, that civilization is an imposed structure and not necessarily something innate to the human condition at all. Even James McAuley had this brought home to him by the landscape, a landscape that strips away what pretense the human has to being civilized, to being buffered by his or her culture from barbarity, because the very air contains a "faint sterility that disheartens and derides." The sea has dried to a "salty sunken desert" and the people are emptied of much human content; yet McAuley adds that "I am fitted to that land as the soul is to the body. . . ."[6]

By terming Australia a "futile heart within a fair periphery," McAuley directly links the physical and psychic worlds that his country represents for many of its artists. Australia has a thin periphery of green near the cities, where the people live. Beyond that is the outback, the bush. Similarly, civilization is a thin veneer and humankind faces the emptiness within, the "faint sterility that disheartens and derides." The outer landscape, utterly alien, becomes the inner landscape, the otherness within

the human mind: "Voyage within you, on the fabled ocean, / And you will find that Southern Continent . . . mythical Australia."[7]

Yet, paradoxically, this barrenness can foster a sense of community; a correspondence between the strange land and the estranged people is not merely negative. Judith Wright comments: "Australia has from the beginning of its short history meant something more to its new inhabitants than mere land to be occupied, ploughed and brought into subjection. It has been the outer equivalent of an inner reality; first, and persistently, the reality of exile; second . . . the reality of newness and freedom."[8] This, if not the other side of the coin, does bespeak a different mintage. Whereas McAuley found the Australians independent but not free, Wright has found the very enormity of Australia to be liberating. The intemperate climate and landscape may expose humans to their own barrenness, but it also creates a social bonding; it is from the challenge of the environment that the peculiarly Australian ideal of *mateship* springs. Wright offers what she believes to be a fundamental difference between Australia and America: "Where the American dream made use of the competitive individualistic element in life . . . the Australian dream emphasizes man's duty to his brother, and man's basic equality, the mutual trust which is the force that makes society cohere" (Wright 1966, xxi–xxii). The hostility of the environment has created the "force that makes society cohere." This would seem to be just the opposite approach from McAuley's poem: to Wright, the futile heart has metaphorically created the fair periphery, the savageness of the land has helped foster the graces of civilization.

But this is to treat the situation a bit too broadly, because there are many disquieting elements in Judith Wright's vision as well. As the land forces itself into the mind of its inhabitants, so did the white invaders force themselves onto the land. Wright points out that the aborigines "were bound to the land we took from them, by the indissoluble link of religion and totemic worship, so that our intrusion on the land itself became a kind of bloodless murder, even where no actual murder took place" (Wright 1966, xvii). The very presence of the white race is an act of psychic violence, although European consciousness of this fact grew slowly. The Australian of European descent faces the collective guilt felt by Americans: the land was conquered at the terrible expense of the native population. Although there may be something self-serving in the postmodern *mea culpa*, it is true that attitudes, however subconsciously they may live on, do not necessarily die with the people who originally

held them. For Wright, as well as for many other Australian writers, violence, brutality, and barbarity exist underneath the social bond, the mateship that is viewed as uniquely Australian.

This awareness results in a certain estrangement from the land. In her poem "At Cooloola," Judith Wright notes first the utter indifference of the landscape, how the "blue crane fishing in Cooloola's twilight / has fished there longer than our centuries," while the poet is a "stranger, come of a conquering people" who cannot share in the calm, "being unloved by all my eyes delight in." Then she senses that the land is still at heart the land of the aborigines and the "invader's feet will tangle / in nets there and his blood be thinned by fears." The landscape threatens the supposed conqueror: "I am challenged by a drift-wood spear" and "must quiet a heart accused by its own fear."[9] Earth is spirit; the heart has its own fear. Even for Judith Wright, one of her land's leading environmentalists and one of the best poets her country has thus far produced, the land is sinister in many of its aspects.

The critic who has stated this thesis most explicitly is Harry Heseltine in his essay "Australian Image: The Literary Heritage." Heseltine claims that the democratic theme, while significant, is not the center of the Australian imagination. Rather, he holds that "Australia's literary heritage is based on a unique combination of glances into the pit and the erection of safety fences to prevent any toppling in."[10] And he is not alone in this view; another critic, Alec King, wrote that Australian irony "is a kind of defence . . . inevitable perhaps in a transplanted people face to face with the unhomely enormity of our oversize and intemperate continent."[11]

Heseltine then adapts the conception of Nietzsche and Trilling, that the social order is based on cruelty, to the Australian scene. We have already seen a variation of this idea implicit in Judith Wright's work and need only to recall what is perhaps the best-known fact about modern Australia: it began as a penal colony—the entire continent was one huge jail. Human society, the thin veneer, is another safety fence: "Society is an act, a decent bluff, which makes bearable the final emptiness, the nothingness of the honestly experienced inner life" (304). Mateship is a hedge against this nothingness and was important in a frontier society in which sheer physical survival was an overwhelming preoccupation. Only in a more advanced civilization, ironically, can we afford to sit back and ponder that "sense of the horror of sheer existence" (307). But, according to Heseltine, it is the awareness of this horror that gives Australian writing its unique force: "A feature of a good deal of recent Aus-

tralian writing has been its willingness to use an exploration of the bush as an analogy for the exploration of the individual soul. Just as at the heart of the continent is a burning, insane emptiness, so too at the heart of a man is the horror of his prehistory" (308).

Irrationality, Heseltine points out, is not only at the core of the continent but is at the heart of the actual discovery of the country. At the beginning of Kenneth Slessor's "Five Visions of Captain Cook," the winds cry "choose" to the explorers Tasman and Bougainville. They displayed prudence and went northward with the winds and did not discover Australia, while Cook chose to go "Over the brink, into the devil's mouth" with the result that today "men write poems in Australia."[12] It is this going "over the brink, into the devil's mouth" that gives birth to Australian poetry.

To end with this viewpoint, however, is to fall into the trap of nihilism, which, while often a convenient critical position, simplifies a more complex reality. Cook's choice may have seemed madness, but it gave birth to a nation and a poetry. The bush may offer a dark vision, but more and more the major Australian poets attempt to go to the core of this darkness and then transcend it.

As Heseltine points out, the early writers attempted to beat around the bush, as it were; when these writers "did confront the heart of the matter, it was usually in the form of an attempt to physically subdue the bush and so control its power to subvert the mind" (306). But a subtle shift takes place in the mind of the modern poet who deals with the outback. I've already quoted extensively from McAuley's "Envoi" with its "sterility" and "futile heart." However, once the speaker in the poem accepts his or her identity with the land, accepts that the physical landscape is also a spiritual landscape, the speaker proclaims "its triumphs are my own" and concludes that "Beauty is order and good chance in the artesian heart" though the "reluctant and uneasy land [may] resent / The gush of waters, the lean plough, the fretful seed" (216). The heart is now artesian, and there is hidden life in the center, however grudgingly the soil and soul admit it.

With this perspective, creation remains possible and possibly affirmative. One cannot write unendingly of nothingness, but when one can affirm in the face of great doubt, then the poetry is strengthened because of that very doubt. In much the same way, one's spirituality is strengthened after the dark night of the soul. And this allows for a further shift in Australian poetry: a different sort of relationship with the land becomes possible, one that would have been unthinkable before,

say, 1940. The bush, though still dangerous and nearly as mysterious, is seen as vulnerable. The technology that has made life on the whole comfortable in Australia is also threatening the landscape. It is perhaps a statement on the fragility of human life that we are almost always able to feel more of a sense of identification with that which is weaker or threatened than that which appears triumphant. Judith Wright, in her poem "Australia 1970," addresses her land: "Die, wild country, like the eagle hawk, / dangerous till the last breath's gone." The humans are "conquerors and self-poisoners . . . dying of the venoms that we make / even while you die of us. . . . we are ruined by the thing we kill" (Wright 1978, 126).

Which brings us back to A. D. Hope. Following a discussion regarding the overpowering aspect of the Australian landscape, how it has permeated the conscious and unconscious creative mind, it might seem odd to have to establish Hope's claim to nationality, whether Hope is really an Australian poet or a marooned Anglophile. But we must take time for just such a consideration.

Hope himself must be held partly to blame for the raising of the question. Writing his pamphlet "Australian Literature 1950–1962," Hope claims: "Comment on his own poems by the writer of this pamphlet would be out of place, but his apparent indifference to Australian themes perhaps illustrates by contrast how deeply involved in their surroundings are most other Australian poets of the day."[13] A critic as perceptive as Leonie Kramer sounds the same theme a decade and a half later: "The omission from *The Wandering Islands* of the poem 'Australia' emphasizes how little interested Hope has been in his own country as a subject for poetry. Of the prominent post-war poets . . . he has been the least influenced by distinctively Australian experience."[14] (I shall consider a more plausible reason for the omission of "Australia" in a few paragraphs.)

In most of his work, Hope does not seem to be writing about Australia in any explicit, overt way. But one does not have to be a Jindyworobak to be faithful to one's roots in the Australian experience. Being a poet in the Antipodes created certain tensions, especially in Hope's youth. In *The New Cratylus,* Hope writes "Romantic mentors had convinced me that poetry should above all be richly poetical, but to achieve this I had to use a vocabulary which would not fit the Australian scene." He then goes on to quote Tennyson's famous lines "The woods decay, the woods decay and fall / The vapours weep their burthen to the ground, / Man comes and tills the field" and comments that these lines

had the "elevation, the tone, what Matthew Arnold had called the 'high seriousness' of poetry." Hope then tries to imagine the lines as they might be written in Australia: "The bush decays, the bush decays and falls / The damp fogs wrap their loads upon the ground / Man comes and ploughs the paddock" and sadly comments "No, it would not do." Hope cites Keats's "Ode to a Nightingale" as an example of a poem whose "pure lyric note [is set] in the title itself but 'Ode to a Mopoke' . . . had something inherently ridiculous about it."[15]

Hope, McAuley, and Douglas Stewart were lumped together by most Australian critics of their day into the general grouping "academic poets," which was an attempt to render them irrelevant by those seeking a distinctively Australian idiom. Yet Hope has proven to be much more of a lasting force in his country than any of the Jindyworobaks. Talent has a great deal to do with this, but we can find just how Australian Hope really is if we look past the smoke screen of labels and generalities, most of which have more basis in literary politics than in poetics.

William Walsh noted that "Hope's 'conservatism' in fact is truly radical. His poetry had to be freed from the influence of home, from a tradition still too much domesticated within the nineteenth century."[16] And it is true that most nineteenth-century Australian poetry was watered-down Wordsworth, incongruous in the bush. Oftentimes, a British colony will preserve English ways no longer in use even in Britain. Such an approach is as inherently dishonest as was the contention from the Jindyworobaks that poets should look to the aborigine rather than the English tradition for their roots. The white race, though it may have stolen the aborigines' land, has certainly not inherited their culture. England offers a parallel. Literature in English has itself a European base but does not really descend from the original conquerors of Britain; rather, it is most rooted in classical and Judeo-Christian linguistic soil. Thus Australian poetry in the English language owes its allegiance to these sources and is firmly fixed in the European tradition.[17]

As I stated previously, poetry in English is English poetry, with regional differences. Usually, the more overt these regional differences, the more they're stressed, the more provincial and limited the poem. Hope remarked in a 1986 interview that "Regionalism is like the air we breathe; it is all around us and so we do not need to promote it. I count myself and Les Murray as regional poets because we live and write in Australia, not because we adopt any particular attitude to the country or its language or its society."[18]

Despite this, Leonie Kramer still claims that "as a poet Hope has claimed no nationality, and made no attempt to reflect the particular society and the environment in which he has lived all but a small part of his life." Yet Kramer does allow that within the "body of his poems" there is "an intense preoccupation with landscape" (8). Whatever the critics or Hope may say, it is the poems that will determine Hope's relationship with his land, and it is to these that we must now turn.

A poem such as "Australia" seems an exception in Hope's early work in that it deals explicitly with the Australian locale, but it is actually central to his concerns. The land is a "Nation of trees, drab green and desolate grey / In the field uniform of modern wars" and her ruins are not those of a civilization known by the white race but are the "endless outstretched paws / Of Sphinx demolished or stone lion worn away." He then debunks the myth of Australia being a youthful land of opportunity, which would compensate for the lack of a tradition, by calling it the "last of lands, the emptiest" lacking "songs, architecture, history. . . ." There is nothing here of McAuley's "artesian heart." The population is composed of "monotonous tribes," of "ultimate men" whose "boast is not 'we live' but 'we survive', / A type who will inhabit the dying earth." The cities are termed "five teeming sores" filled with "second-hand Europeans."

So far the picture is uniformly grim, not the sort of description that would please the tourism board. But there is both a subtle and substantial change in the concluding two stanzas in which the speaker acknowledges that he prefers such a landscape, a desert that may still breed prophets, to "the lush jungle of modern thought"; perhaps such a primitive land may avoid the "learned doubt, the chatter of cultured apes" that the rest of the Western world suffers under the guise of civilization. Suddenly we become aware that the poem is a homecoming, that the outstretched paws of the sphinx may be an ambiguous welcome. It is from that barrenness, that Old Testament aridity, that prophets *may* spring; modern thought may be a "lush jungle," but such a jungle is capable only of producing "the chatter of cultured apes." Australia is a wilderness that needs a voice. The poet thus has a prophetic role to play: to make mysteries known, to perform a social function.[19]

As Kramer pointed out, Hope did not print "Australia" in *The Wandering Islands,* although he has subsequently printed the poem in all the editions of his collected poems. I do not believe that he left the poem out of *The Wandering Islands* to show how unaffected he was by his surroundings but rather because he found the negative view perhaps too overstated. Hope spoke of the poem in that same 1986 interview and

remarked that he just "came back from England. I was out of a job, I hadn't done very well in my studies overseas, and it was a pretty miserable time anyway in the middle of the Great Depression." He remarks that the positive aspects of the poem come from 1939. Besides, he is a bit tired of the poem: "I sometimes say that that poem follows me round like a bad smell" (Kuch 229–30). The final two verses were written nine years after the poem was originally conceived. That Hope has continued to print the poem despite his reservations about it is most probably simply because it's an excellent poem, but he clearly does not want it read as his definitive view of Australia. What Hope rejects is not Australia but provincialism.

In fact, Hope displays in his poetry many of the reactions to his environment that we have seen evidenced by other Australian poets. The image of the desert as a place of power permeates his work: "The lion in deserts royally takes his prey; / Gaunt crags cast back the hunting eagle's scream" (*CP,* 99). The desert metaphor recurs when Hope speaks of heroes: "This is their image: the desert and the wild . . ." (*CP,* 67). There is also a strong sense in Hope of what I have termed previously the thin veneer, the darkness always ready to break through, a major theme that must occupy its own chapter.

Ross Mezger has noted another use of landscape by Hope, a usage particularly suited to the Australian outback: "The deliberate, symbolic use of landscape images places the person in a disordered, non-realistic world where he is unable to experience the creative redemptive aspects of love."[20] This is the province of frustrated passion. For example, in "The Damnation of Byron," the hero wanders in his own special hell, a "landscape of erotic dreams" in which the "cactus or euphorbia here and there / Thrusts up its monstrous phallus at the sky" (*CP,* 2). Similarly, in another poem, "The Dream," two lovers look into each other's eyes and see "the vast / Deserts of sand" and hear a maelstrom of "Voices of pleading or insane abuse . . ." (*CP,* 52).

Just as the life in the desert must drink from secret springs, so must the miracle of creative life. In "An Epistle from Holofernes," Holofernes speaks of a "healing language from the mouths of death" that in the past "would have been a magic rod whose blow / Broke the parched rocks and made their waters flow," finding beneath the desert the "Layers of water [that] lie beneath that ground," waters that succor "our Forbidden Tree" (*CP,* 58).

The tree motif is found again in "The Gateway," where the "tree through the stiff clay at long last forces / Its thin strong roots and taps

the secret spring." This too is a poem about homecoming: "Here I come home: in this expected country / They know my name and speak it with delight" (*CP,* 25). In a sense, the landscape is transformed into the body of love.

It is but a short move, as shall be seen in later chapters, from the sensuality of "The Gateway" to considerations of art; art and sex are both creative acts, though the miracle of creation is ambiguous. In "Flower Poem," the poem, the plant, "Achieves its miracle from soil and wind, / Rooted in dung, dirt, dead men's bones. . . ." The actual source of the admired flower is primordial, sensual, and dangerous; plunging deep through the forbidding levels of earth, the poem "penetrates the cave beneath" to where the "subterranean river roars," the realm of the troll where the "the grinning girls / Sit spinning the bright fibre of their sex" (*CP,* 14). We are here at the root of myth, that which forces the sphinx through the sands.

Another natural image recurring in Hope's work that correlates to the Australian scene is the island. Hope's youth was spent on Tasmania, and the title of his first collection was *The Wandering Islands.* The title poem is a strangely flawed piece. It is a reversal of Donne's statement that no person is an island, but it demonstrates a confusion in imagery most uncommon in Hope. The poem begins "You cannot build bridges between the wandering islands; / The Mind has no neighbours" (*CP,* 26), and the verses that follow establish the islands as a metaphor for the individual who can make no real connection with another person. However, when verse four states that these islands are a "refuge only for the ship-wrecked sailor," the imagery becomes muddled.

A more successful example of this motif is "The Drifting Continent." The speaker is picnicking with "a female of my kind" in the outback and "the ancient land" focused on the "arid earth, the history / Of its archaic inhabitants adrift." The continent itself becomes an enormous, slowly moving raft, drifting at the rate of two centimeters a year. The picnickers have a meeting with an anteater that passes by, one of the two surviving types of monotreme, the other being the duck-billed platypus. Gradually, they become aware that they are the recent intruders on the Australian raft and that, though they have each other, they are the ones who are lost. By the poem's end the two are still able to laugh, "but with a deep and growing unease," feeling they were mere "ciphers in a species bound for death."[21]

As we shall see throughout Hope's work, two anodynes against this isolation are love and art. In his moving elegy "In Memoriam: James

Philip McAuley, 1976," Hope mentions McAuley's removal to Tasmania a short time before his death, how the landscape "Took root in [McAuley's] poetry." And then he notes his own roots in Tasmania, his "boyhood's home, / My 'land of similes' " (*Ant,* 16). In art, a sense of community, however fragile, can exist; but lacking that communal tie, the sense of horror that Heseltine writes of asserts itself, as in the recollections of "Ascent into Hell." Here Hope recalls his island youth and finds "Memory no more the backward, solid continent, / From island to island of despairing dream" (*CP,* 31).

Another element Hope shares with many Australian poets is a strong ecological sense. One of the earliest examples of this concern is his satirical piece, "Toast for a Golden Age," in which a "middle-aged, middle-brow male of the middle-class" is toasted "as type of the human race." Humanity's "triumphs of reason" are ironically honored; the "Earth, our mother, at last has found a master" who "made the old girl work faster, / Stripping her naked and shouting to make her run." By the end of the poem, the human misses the bus announced by Time as "he gropes in his heart, in his hat, in his fourteen pockets, / But the ticket is missing— the ticket has never been there" (*CP,* 85). "On an Early Photograph of My Mother" largely reworks the same turf, though not as successfully. Hope has also surprised readers late in his career by writing a number of poems, somewhat reminiscent of the popular balladeer Banjo Patterson, praising the beauties of the Australian landscape.

There is a considerable difference in tone from "Australia" to the later, elegiac, "Beyond Khancoban," with its loving return to the land; as Hope drives, "the brooding landscape comes alive," and he finds he is "turning its world into music" as he travels. Here the final stanza is one of the most succinct statements on the real worth of regionalism, one certainly more valuable than any made by the Jindyworobaks: he senses his own elemental roots in this landscape, "the place where a mind began / Able to offer itself to the galaxies" (*Ant,* 3). Hope's real argument, the butt of his satire, is not with Australia *per se* but with the modern exploitation of the natural world and human sensibility.

Chapter Two
The Satiric

Readers delving into an essay entitled "The Discursive Mode" in Hope's prose collection *The Cave and the Spring* probably would not expect to find themselves launched into a discussion of ecology, but that is what they find. Hope writes of deserts he has seen in Australia, including one in South Australia caused by the introduction of the goat and the rabbit. He goes on to state that there is an "analogous destruction of the landscape of literature by the intrusion of alien and cheap forms of sterile amusement" and that literary history evidences a "slow progress towards a desert ecology from the sixteenth century to the present day." Hope laments the disappearance of the epic, the great philosophical poem, the verse tragedy, the "verse satire, the ode, the epistle, the elegy, the romance, the hortatory or instructive poem, the pastoral and the long meditative poem or celebrant hymn," as well as the "innumerable lowlier forms of sonnet or epigram and song."

Hope finds that this multitude of forms has been replaced with "the sparse and monotonous vegetation of the arid steppe: little poems of reflection, brief comments, interior monologues, sharp critical barks and hisses, songs that never become articulate; earnestness that lacks the enchantment of truth, and frivolity that disgusts by its absence of charm."[1] He sees the development of the novel, which usurped the lengthy verse narrative, as one of the earliest signs of decline.

Since novels are inevitably more pedestrian than verse epics, and more solicitous of the popular mind, the expectations a reader has of literature become diminished. This eventually produces a similar diminishment in mind and vision, an enfeeblement of spirit; what's lost is not just a literary form but the capacity for the fullest human response. Hope remarks that a "certain nobility of mind was lost with the passing of epic. . . . real magnanimity was lost with tragedy" and the "attitudes of mind and heart . . . died out as they ceased to be practiced." Because of this impoverishment, poets and readers were "unable any longer to understand what they had lost, or indeed what was meant by a 'form' at all" (*Cave,* 4). Hope goes on to make the additional point that since the moderns have lost all feeling for the innate nature of forms, choices

that "tremble on the limits of sensibility," the cultured sense of rightness
of an active tradition seem to the contemporary mind to be purely arbitrary.

Whether one accepts Hope's argument *in toto,* it seems irrefutable
that forms that once seemed natural, ones that seemed at the disposal of
the gifted artist, now appear altogether inappropriate, with no comparable mode to take their place. It is true that certain forms flourish at particular times because they address the concerns and historical impera-
tives of a particular age. Attempts at reviving these forms usually seem
futile exercises, curious efforts doomed to fail from the start unless they
can be retooled and revitalized. Certainly a poet of genius such as Auden
illustrates that most forms don't die—they remain moribund until
genius and circumstance combine to resurrect them.

Hope returns to his ecological analogy to suggest methods of reviving the grander forms. One cannot plant a great redwood in the desert;
the soil needs to be restored with lesser forms of vegetation that can prepare the earth. He points out that the "first step in intelligent regenera-
tion of the soil of poetry may well be to re-establish the discursive mode,
in particular to restore the practice of formal satire" and adds that
"wherever the golden derision or the *saeva indignatio* of satire strikes, it
weakens and shakes the forces that corrupt the heart and destroy
poetry" (*Cave,* 9).

But this raises another difficulty for the critical modern temper.
Almost all critics agree that epic is a majestic form, though it seems, for
a variety of reasons, no longer appropriate for our time. While it is true
that the last decade has seen a number of book-length poems published,
most tend to be novelistic rather than epic; attempts to create a modern
epic by such poets as Derek Walcott and Frederick Turner, while including some brilliant passages, tend to lack the staying power, the inner
momentum of the great epics. And there has been even less effort to
revive satire, although contemporary poets such as James Fenton and R.
S. Gwynn have written some very fine satire indeed.

For the past two centuries satire has been deemed inferior to the lyric,
today's dominant poetic form. Hope's own efforts in satire have met
with critical reserve. The Australian critic Cecil Hadgraft leaves no
doubt he considers satire itself an inferior form: "Since mere diatribe or
invective is not in question but rather polished and acid comment, the
adept user of the weapon has needed skill. So that we can think of these
poets for the most part as technicians" (198). By inference, these are not
real poets at all, quite a strange critical comment for Hadgraft to make,

much like Arnold calling Pope a master of English prose. If that which
requires skill makes its user a technician "for the most part," then the
truest poet would be one who displayed no skill whatsoever. While this
may be true of much contemporary poetry, it has rarely been so honestly
stated.

Yet more gifted critics than Hadgraft share his reservations about
satire. Vincent Buckley claims that satire is "not only inferior as a genre,
it is not the most suited to Hope's particular talent" (151). Before considering Hope's abilities and liabilities as a satirist, these claims about
satire as a mode need to be explored.

Hope himself admits that his students "can be led quite easily to
enjoy good satire, its wit, its farce, its ridicule, its invective, its serious
intention. But ask them to discuss it as *poetry* and they find it lacking
precisely in the feeling they associate with poetry" (*Cave,* 62). Hope
explores several possible reasons. We still are, after all, the heirs of the
romantics, though not of Byron. Byron is the romantic poet Hope most
closely resembles in sensibility and Byron remains something of an
anomaly: though he was the quintessential romantic hero to the popular
mind, he was actually the romantic poet who had the most in common
with the eighteenth century. It is impossible to conceive of Wordsworth
writing *Don Juan*. The popular image of the poet has become the dying
Keats or the boozing Dylan Thomas—tragic rather than satiric figures.
Satire also unabashedly extols a particular point of view, which is anath-
ema to the modernist poetic ethos.

While all this may be true, the primary reason for this dismissal of
satire is apparent, I think, in Hope's very defense of it: "Satire as the
voice of public opinion has a social function that places it on a level with
Religion, Law, and Government. Though its tone may be light, its function is wholly serious; and as for passion it is activated by a fierce and
strenuous moral and intellectual enthusiasm, the passion for order, justice, and beauty" (*Cave,* 62). The reason for satire's decline in the present
is the same as the justification of its success in the past. Poetry today has
no social function; those few individuals who still approach poetry at all
do not do so from motives of social reparation. For nearly two centuries
the vatic nature of poetry has been emphasized at the expense of the
civic. This is not to say that Pope was a best-seller in his day; but a poet
did have a voice with the literate audience. One has only to read of the
heated arguments—discussions would probably be too polite a term—
carried on in the press of the day to realize that a writer such as Pope
had an audience, if not actually an influence. Satire, more than any other

mode of poetry, needs an audience, while the contemporary lyric all too often seems bred in solipsism.

There is the additional difficulty of satire being a generally aristocratic pursuit. Hope remarks that he thinks the major reason the poet does not write satire today is because of "an obscure feeling that he should not set himself up as a man with superior intellectual standards, superior taste or morals to his fellow men, to tell them that nine-tenths of them have minds that prefer garbage and to make fun of them at their grisly troughs" (*Cave,* 67). Since Hope has written much satire, especially up to his middle age, it can be safely assumed he has not suffered from these compunctions.

It is just this spirit of commercialism, this creation of arbitrary needs and cheapening of thought and action, that often raised Hope to his most invective satire. Indeed, commercialism is so insidious that it should be a subject for poetry, and its civic nature would seem to make it an appropriate target for satire.

The poem "Standardization" (*CP,* 10) is one of Hope's best-known complaints about modern life, though it has uncertain aim. The poem opens with a journalist "brooding on this Modern Age" and with his "marketable woes" and "fatuous, flatulent, Sunday-paper prose" filling up his "inevitable page." Other types are soon parodied: a "green aesthete starts to whoop / With horror at the house not made with hands" and is soon followed by "another pure theosophist" and "still one more Nature poet." At this point, he comes up with a daring strategy—for all his supposed poetic conservatism Hope has never been reluctant to take chances—that both lifts the poem out of the ordinary and causes substantial problems for it as a work of art.

After dispensing with these doomsayers, the poet sees the "old, sound Earth" and claims "is no manufacturer competes / With her in the mass production of shapes and things," that the same patterns are endlessly re-created. This is both a clever and insightful ploy that stands expectation on its head, but Hope commits a mistake nearly fatal to the poem. Vivian Smith is correct when he states that the "aim is not as accurate as the tone would have us believe, and Hope is obscuring the target rather than hitting it. The aesthete's objection is not to natural conformity but to a mechanical stereotype. The potter, like nature, is constantly producing the same shape, but each jug has its own evolution and variation within this uniformity, unlike a mass-production plastic jug."[2] The poem's strategy is effective, but it is unfair, much like the typical political speech that blames a certain class, which may be eminently culpable

for some other transgression, for something with which it had nothing to do. The repetitions of nature are life enhancing, whereas the shoddiness of modern mass production honors only its own obsolescence, its sterile monotony. It is a pity that the poem is in this way dishonest, because there is much to admire about it.

"The Bed" (*CP*, 17) is a more successful poem, perhaps because its tone is more controlled. In fact, it is something of an exercise in gallows humor in which the "patient loves his bed" because it is both the place of birth and death. In this best of all possible worlds, there is much love to be shared between doctor and patient and patient and "patient bed." The bed, too, "adores the doctor" whose "cool and skilful touch" will bring it more of the dying. The tone is perfect here, something Hope has trouble sustaining in his less successful satires.

The lightness of the poet's touch, which at first obscures the darkness of the subject, makes the theme all the more horrific by its seeming inappropriateness. Tone in satire is effective if it is lighter than the subject with which it deals; if it is heavier, it seems a ranting out of all proportion with the topic. Strangely, even satire that takes the form of burlesque or farce benefits from understatement. Anger must be sublimated to wit. A poem such as "A Commination" (*CP*, 148) comes, for me, too close to ranting, though I can certainly understand the scorn Hope feels for the types he labels as "Drivellers, snivellers, writers of bad verse" and "Small turds from the great arse of self-esteem." Hope particularly focuses on advertising professionals, comparing them to pimps.

One can take a certain pleasure in his anger, but that's just where the problem lies: this sort of invective is too self-indulgent. One senses the rage of the wounded more than the absurdity of the buffoons whose actions prompted the poem. Pope was a master of insult, but the reader rarely if ever senses that Pope is barely keeping his temper under control. Rather, the poet is always cool, the one sane individual amidst all the nonsense being described. Still, there is something I like about "A Commination," especially the damnation to which the culprits are sentenced: to watch television till their minds become a "flaccid mass of phototropic cells." While I can see Hope's point, I am uneasy as to the judgment of the speaker; indeed, the persona is aware of the danger that he's running. In the last verse, he asks to be led away from Sodom "lest with them I learn to gibber and gloat." It seems, alas, too late to avoid this fate.

"Meditation Music" (*CP*, 27) is an attack on the medium of radio, a poem also uneven in tone and not as successful as "A Commination,"

though there are some very nice lines: "Latter day miracles are in reverse: / The Flesh is now made Word for all to hear." "The Brides" (*CP,* 82) satirizes our infatuation with the automobile, "every inch a wife." "Letter from the Line" (*CP,* 151) is a generally successful piece satirizing America, which the speaker characterizes as a place where "the supermarket dictates the range of desire / And the passions are packaged." But these observations are then balanced with a humanness that makes his caustic remarks seem all the more true because they are not made out of bitterness: "but of course such observations are silly," the speaker allows, adding that a "whale doesn't look his best when you travel inside." There is real affection in the closing lines for those whom he has left behind. It is a successful poem; however, the satire is saved because the criticism is mixed with a sense of regret that redeems the poem but keeps it from strict adherence to the satiric mode. Erring on the side of generosity, while harming the unity of the poem, tempers criticism with affection and adds an element of believability.

Religion is always fallow ground for the satirist, as it is for Hope, himself a minister's son. But "Heldensagen" (*CP,* 21) and "Morning Coffee" (*CP,* 24) are simply too obscure to work as satire, their allusive puns and analogies remote from the ordinary reader's experience. Here Hope is being too clever; a man of great erudition, his learning is usually beneficial to his poetry, but at times, as here, can seem a willful intellectual obscurantism. For example, in "Morning Coffee" he not only succumbs to the dreadful pun "strip teas" but refers to "temporary Tantalus" who is "Suckled on Jungfraumilch" and witnesses a "mock Sabellian rape," the last referring to the Sabine women and the early Church heretic Sabellius, if not more. Good satire has immediate sting. In these two poems a reader soon is overcome by a feeling that the rewards they give are just not worth the effort they require; the economic law of diminishing returns cheapens its intellectual wares.

"The Martyrdom of Saint Teresa" (*CP,* 63) is an interesting poem that parodies the cult of religious relics; its subject nearly justifies the brutality of the poem in which the "little nuns of her foundation" compete for "an elbow, or the heart" from the saints' butcher shop. It is remarkably effective, in a grisly way, but one might have a reservation as to its timeliness. The age of religious relics has passed. Such a poem a few centuries ago might have earned Hope his own martyrdom; now, while it is a memorable poem, its concern seems antiquated.

"The House of God" (*CP,* 51) captures well the mock piety that oozes from many churches; while this theme is a fairly easy target, Hope's aim

is sure. Here the worshipers are cats who "Twine and rub against [God's] shins" apologizing for the stolen piece of fish or a scrap with the dog. God finally takes pity and releases a shower of little mice from his beard.

The trendier absurdities of modern psychology are as vulnerable a target as the false pieties of religion. In "The Return from the Freudian Islands" (*CP*, 18) Hope attacks the psychoanalytic community head-on. In the poem, when the inhabitants of the Freudian Islands first heard of "Sigmund the Saviour" they were so impressed they "abandoned the worship of their fathers' ghosts." Sigmund revealed to them how they suffered from the "disease of sin" by keeping their bodies "morbidly concealed," so nudity became the costume of the day, despite the coldness of the climate. Stripped in their "Brave Nude World" they soon found their nakedness insufficient, and it was not long before the "first skinned girl walked primly down the street."

This reductionism continues until the "skinned men blushed to see the skeleton." Hope pulls no punches in a graphic description of the results; the body is described at length in considerable and revolting detail. One is reminded of Swift's minute description of marketing in "A Modest Proposal." But this is the last straw—things have gone too far, and finally "a poet buttoned on his skin." It is the poet who calls the community back to its senses, who affirms our humanity against the reductive analysis of the psyche.

Yet Hope himself was a student of psychological analysis and had training as a vocational psychologist. Why was Freud such a target? Kevin Hart is accurate when he writes that "One reason Hope deals so harshly with Freud is because psychoanalysis and poetry contest the same space, the world of dreams and myths."[3] Hope's antagonism is thus a battle over turf. Jung would be more congenial to Hope's mythologizing imagination than would Freud. However, Freud is frequently too tempting for Hope—both are more preoccupied with exploring the sexual wilderness than is Jung.

And sex is a frequent object of Hope's satire. "Sportsfield" (*CP*, 80) details a sexual Olympics in which professional lovers engage in sex before a coliseum packed with "amateurs who practise in parked cars." The sport itself most resembles soccer, but the poem is harmed by its ending; the last two verses drop the narrative structure and the speaker intrudes to moralize, ending with an invocation to the "Goddess of kind." The final two stanzas contain some wonderful lines but are not fitting with the rest of the poem. Satire usually requires the reasoned

rather than the impassioned voice, and the persona must never doff his or her mask.

"The Explorers" (*CP*, 11) examines the journey through puberty of young girls who wander into the jungle of sexuality, "jungles full of eyes and fears." But when they have successfully maneuvered their way to the "miraculous clearing," they win a "little brick cottage, the ration of lawn in front / And a kiss at the gate and a pair of trousers walking daily to the office." However, Hope's two finest satires dealing with sexual matters are "The Lingam and the Yoni" (*CP*, 39) and "Conquistador" (*CP*, 34).

The lingam and the yoni, the male and female principles, are joined together, but they must deal with modern society, the diurnal cares that people must confront while living happily ever after. In "The Lingam and the Yoni," their conversation is diminished to concerns of neighborhood and payment on the furniture. Finally, they are able to buy their "box of brick," but it "makes her prisoner." The woman is kept like a possession and the male, though dominant, is forced to become a wage slave. They pay their "haemorrhage of rent" and borrow "Against the heart," and in their bookkeeping they "count what they destroy." This is a superb statement on the modern concerns that destroy love, and the poem is accomplished with a lightness of tone that allows rather than forces the poem to make its point.

Likewise, "Conquistador" is a wonderful poem, simultaneously funny and tragic. In a recent interview, Hope described the genesis of the poem as coming from a combination of his thinking of John Crowe Ransom's "Captain Carpenter" and observing a man in a lounge getting up his nerve to approach a single woman sitting down the bar from him (Kuch 222). This mingling of literary sources and observed experience is typical of Hope. In his poem, this incident became the story of Henry Clay. The name is important in itself. Clay is of course easily reshaped, and Hope would also be aware that the historical American figure Henry Clay was known as the Great Compromiser. The Henry Clay of "Conquistador" is certainly a compromised character.

Henry is "a small man in a little way" who one day goes to a hotel lounge, a "most unusual place for him to go." There he meets the girl who was so large that Henry "gave the waiter twice the usual tip." Henry immediately starts to have grandiose visions of what's to come and experiences an interesting assortment of fantasies, all while still at the bar. He and the woman drink till closing time and then take the tram to her place; while on the train Henry hears the sky blare "with its

grand orchestral voice / The Gotterdammerung of Henry Clay." When
they go to bed Henry senses that "his Moment looked him in the face,"
and Henry "rose to meet it as a hero must." However, Henry, like all
true heroes, meets his demise just after his greatest victory, for "The
enormous girl rolled over and squashed him flat" and turned him into a
"bedside mat."

This is Hope's finest satirical portrayal of what becomes an almost
obsessive theme, especially through midcareer: the devouring female
sexual presence that overwhelms the male. "Conquistador" contains
some of the few places in his satire that Hope sustains a lightness of tone
and sufficient distance while dealing with this subject.

Vivian Smith wrote that "Hope's approach, in his satirical pieces, is
militant; he reduces and deflates in order to show things in their proper
perspective" (372). That seems to be literally true here. The modern
hero is small—and not much of a match for his heroine. It's a common
enough theme, but what a wonderful travesty of a poem!

Art has always been a major concern of satire, and Hope has many
poems dealing with the arts; surprisingly, though, he has written very
little of a satirical nature about poetry. Still, one of his efforts in this vein
is also his longest poem. *Dunciad Minor* is a mock heroic epic of 6 cantos
and 83 pages. It deals with the state of literary criticism around 1950
and in some aspects seems dated in a way that Pope rarely is. This is not
just because the more extreme claims of the poststructuralists have
made the previous theories seem tame. The theme of the *Dunciad* needs
a stronger narrative to keep its interest alive. It is, of course, modeled on
Pope, but the narrative flow has little of the master's force. The poem
has moments when it is very entertaining, but there are no events as
memorable as those in, say, "The Return from the Freudian Islands" or
"Conquistador."

The work was occasioned by an exchange with a romantic scholar, A.
A. Phillips, who debunked Pope on a literary radio program. There was
a Phillips in Pope's *Dunciad,* so Hope updated the work to include the
present Phillips. The poem was written from a quite legitimate concern
that Hope had expressed in the essay "Literature versus the Universities"
from his prose collection *The Cave and the Spring*: "with the great pres-
tige of English studies in American universities, literary criticism which
has once been the handmaid of literature was fast becoming the mistress" (178). Judging from the rancor of much of the piece, one wishes
that Hope had had the deconstructionists around when he was writing
this poem: he says that the "lesser critics of the canine kind / Will lift

their legs where'er they have a mind," while the more ambitious "hoards his drop, and through the town he runs" so that he anoints "Caesar's statue in the public square; / Proud to be seen and hear his fellows cry: / " 'He pissed on Julius Caesar—so will I.' "[4]

A much finer though shorter poem that deals with the effect of the general culture on the writing of poetry is "Persons from Porlock" (*CP,* 104). It was from Porlock that the perhaps apocryphal visitor came who interrupted Coleridge when he was writing "Kubla Khan." Porlock comes to embody middle-class mediocrity in Hope's poem; the poet finds Coleridge fortunate to have been disturbed by Porlock only once and that works such as "The Ancient Mariner" were spared. Then the poet ponders the horrible possibility of what might have been (or perhaps, more accurately, what might not have been) had Porlock claimed Coleridge as a citizen, had the "Teachers from Porlock organised his mind." He would of course have Porlock neighbors and marry the "sweetest girl in Porlock" and breed some Porlockians himself. After putting up with "Eight hours a day of honest Porlock toil," he somehow still sustained the urge to serve more than a part-time Muse. So he leaves Porlock but discovers Porlock has gone with him and he can but write " 'Amid this tumult Kubla heard from far / Voices of Porlock babbling round the bar.' "

I hope to have shown the range of Hope's satire, its peaks and valleys; but where, after all this, does he stand as a satirist? Most critics are inclined to be dismissive of this aspect of his work, but many don't consider satire a serious discipline anyway; others don't think Hope a good satirist. He can be very uneven in this regard. Gustav Cross writes: "Hope's satires too often betray an uncertainty of direction, and his shafts seem loosed indiscriminately at a multiplicity of targets, more in the style of an Elizabethan railer than of the Augustans."[5] But Hope has written a handful of satirical pieces that are very fine. He may be the finest satirist writing in English since Byron; he is certainly in the four or five finest to follow in the intervening century and a half. Nevertheless, it is also true that he has had very little competition in this regard.

Hope is at least unconsciously aware of the difficulty he has had with satire. None of the poems I have quoted or in any way referred to in this chapter have been written since 1959. For a man who called for the poetic soil to be replenished by verse satire, this is a nearly total satiric silence of three decades. His use of the discursive mode during this time has been primarily the leisurely narrative—*The Age of Reason* is a book composed entirely of such efforts. But there has been little published satire.

Vincent Buckley stated that Hope's satires "express a revulsion dis-proportionate to the follies which they attack."[6] There are some fine poems in which this is not the case, but when the satires fail, it is usually for the reason Buckley mentions. Consider "The Kings" (*CP,* 99), which begins by describing how the "lion in deserts royally takes his prey" and contrasts this with "The King of Parasites, delicate, white and blind . . . Dreams out his greedy and imperious dream / Immortal in the bel-lies of mankind" dwelling in "a rich bath of pre-digested soup, / Warm in the pulsing bowel." Hope refers to the tapeworm as "the voluptuous monarch of the gut . . . the prodigious Solitaire" and then goes on to list heroes from former times; past ages may have their sustaining figures, but Hope finds that the parasite is "for our age a symbol to describe / The secret life of Technocratic Man."

I don't offer "The Kings" as a pure example of satire, but it does treat a subject that could have been handled satirically. "The Kings" as it stands is not satirical because the voice is too involved, too angry to establish the distance necessary for effective scorn. Scorn and anger are two very different though related emotions. The satiric pose cloaked in anger rather than aristocratic scorn produces disgust. Satire offers a model, an ideal, a choice, if only by indirection. When the anger is so total, it is no wonder that the aim seems unsure. This leads to a posture that the reader cannot accept without looking upon life in disgust; it is not that satire is inferior as a mode but that anger such as is often mani-fest in Hope's work is too strong for it. Vincent Buckley was correct when he claimed that "we cannot defer to a criticism of human folly which goes so far as to express disgust with life itself" (151). Feelings of this nature can be probed in poetry, can be transcended in verse; in short, they may be the material of art but not of satire. Hope at his best as a satirist is Augustan, as a civic poet who affirms the right path by ridiculing the false; it is only in his failed satires that Vivian Smith is cor-rect in saying that "Hope's satirical vision is inseparable from his use of the macabre and the grotesque" (375).

Chapter Three

The Grotesque

Many critics, especially those outside Australia who are not as familiar with his work, consider Hope a neoclassical poet. This is a misconception for which Hope himself is partly responsible: he has been public about his preference for the eighteenth-century poets over the romantics; his introduction to *Dunciad Minor,* in which he says his viewpoint is "the classic or neo-classic" (viii), is just one instance among many of his claims to Augustan creative ancestry. But the more perceptive among the Australian critics have long realized that this is not quite the case; as Leonie Kramer states, "for all his formalism, his language has far more in common with some kinds of romantic and post-romantic poetry than with the Augustans" (41). I have already examined how satire seems incapable of containing the fury of much of Hope's writing. This emotional response not only often harms his satire but also is far removed from the urbane spirit Hope admires in the Augustans. This in no way diminishes his standing as a serious poet; it simply means he is a different kind of poet than he might perhaps wish himself considered to be.

It was Vincent Buckley who offered the first view of Hope as a poet which was both in-depth and accurate. Writing in 1957, just two years after Hope's first book was published, Buckley noted that "despite his emphasis on reason, Hope is not really a poet of the Enlightenment" (155). In the same essay, Buckley made an analysis that is considered definitive for Hope, at least till midcareer: "Hope is a classical poet whose material is Romantic. . . . He absorbs the world in terms of a sensibility which is unusual, individualistic, even at times unbalanced and anarchistic; but, that world once part of him, it is subjected to the judgement, to the formative influence, of a strong, deliberate, rather heavy mind" (149–50). The material, with all its violence both physical and psychic, makes its way into the poem through the mediation of a strict adherence to form. The form is an intercessor between savage emotion and art.

In the better poems, this tension between form and content can produce work of great power and depth. When the form is too dominant, as is not often the case, the poem can be flat and seem a mere exercise.

When the content is too raw, too little mediated by a refining sensibility, then the form cannot save the poem from its excesses. Some critics find excess the essence of Hope. Neil Corcoran comments that "the almost despairingly violent energy of [his work] seems to me his truest note. . . . his poems often convey, alarmingly, an energy of anger or vituperation or boredom or lust being held in check, with difficulty, by elaborate formal artifice."[1] And William Walsh, in an otherwise favorable chapter on Hope, finds that there is "something nasty, an occasional gratuitous revelling in the garbage-bin and perhaps also the puritan self-hatred to which this is often a clue, in a few of Hope's poems" (130).

I think Walsh is more accurate here than Corcoran; Hope can become self-indulgent in this fashion, but such excess is generally the exception. However, it is undeniable that our sensual natures very often become a battleground in Hope's work; if the whole of his canon could be compared to a cathedral, these poems are clearly his gargoyles. The poem "Rawhead and Bloody Bones" (CP, 41) can be seen as the paradigm instance where Hope has deviated most from his usual corrective course that separates disillusion from disgust. In this work, the "Belly too commits, / By a strange and self abuse, / Chin-chopper's tit-bits, / Meat of his own mint, chews." This is bad writing and twisted syntax such as one rarely finds in Hope, quite apart from the meaning, or, I am tempted to say, meaninglessness. Soul and Body feed on each other until the "Grisly cud falls at last." It is always surprising to discover how poorly good poets can write at times, and also, on occasion, what bad judgment they can show in editing. In fact, the unusually awkward writing here seems to be disgust heaped equally on our physical natures and the craft of poetry, two paths whereby Hope customarily seeks transcendence.

There are other works with which I feel a bit uneasy but that have an undeniable power. "The Dinner" (CP, 49) is a strong poem that takes chances—I am still uncertain how successfully. The poem begins with an elegant dinner shared by two lovers as "grace descends upon the food and wine." But then the speaker sees his lady "bare [her] teeth to bite" and the scene is totally transformed; he perceives the woman as a beast tearing at her prey, that she whom he recently made love to is now revealed as "gorged with death." The comparisons run on to the tiger, the condor, and the "lithe, cold torpedo of the shark." The beloved is seen as part of the blood sacrifice of the whole world, killing "by proxy a whole herd of swine." Thoughts of the slaughterhouse over dinner can quickly turn one to vegetarianism. However, the vision does not end

here: the persona sees a giant and his mate in their primordial cave cooking their meat on the spit. They are savage beings: "Talking in deep, soft, grumbling undertones / They gnaw and crack and suck the marrowy bones." Certainly this is not civilized table chat, though it may be reproduced nightly in countless kitchens around the world. While this primitive couple is clearly in love, the speaker's perspective has been altered and he sees "their human feast / With the doomed comprehension of the beast" and describes his hair as "bristling." The speaker's illuminations reduce him to a bestial state, less advanced than his primitive progenitors; the darkness of the act of physical sustenance is complete, life engulfing life, feeding on itself.

The ultimate irony here is that a poem that reduces one of our most ritualized and festive occasions to the utter barbarity underlying the facade of civilized life should be written in heroic couplets, Pope's favorite form, which was also the dominant form of an age that bore the epithet of reason. Interestingly, William Walsh, whom I quoted previously as sometimes finding Hope's exploration of the grotesque excessive, has no such reservations about this poem; indeed, he finds that the "reductive habit of the scientist, his concern with origins and causes, becomes in Hope's hands an instrument of poetic exploration" (132). Yet there certainly looms very large here a state of disgust at life's conditions.

The logical or empirical structure of this poem is worth noting. It is something of a reductive syllogism that moves further and further from the world of reason into primeval barbarity and madness. Madness does not come from barbarity itself but from the conscious mind grown aware of its own barbarousness. This results in a psychic displacement— the speaker identifies not with his primordial ancestor in the cave but with the meat that ancestor is tearing apart. That same being, through his emergence in the conscious mind of the speaker, is metaphorically tearing away all the veils of culture we wear ever so uneasily over our more elemental selves. "The Dinner" is a powerful poem and more subtle than it appears at first glance when it threatens to become, once the initial shock at first reading subsides, a mere curiosity. Still, it may go too far, reveling in revulsion for its own sake.

I have no such reservations about many of the other poems on this theme in the Hope canon. "X-Ray Photograph" (*CP,* 42) immediately follows "Rawhead and Bloody Bones" in *Collected Poems 1930–1965* but is much more controlled, the subject not outshouted by the tone. On seeing an x-ray of his head, the persona at first admires the physical ren-

dering as object and finds the "bones are calm and beautiful." But when his sense of identity with this object impresses itself upon him ("the face my future wears"), he falls into a despair that poisons all of life and "full of rage and bliss" senses the "deathshead" in the kiss.

Unlike the speaker in "The Dinner" who recoils in horror from life, this persona, paradoxically, attempts to lose himself in sheer physicality, seeking escape through sexual congress: "Deep in your flesh my flesh to thrust / Against a more tremendous fear." That "more tremendous fear" comes from a realization of the reductiveness of the "mathematical abyss." The x-ray "shows my image in the grave," but the mind shows the "emptiness within" and that all meaningful human contact is impossible. The final despair at human connection is the same as found in "The Wandering Islands," but here the imagery is consistent, the direction true, and the tone under tight control. However, the act of love shares a masturbatory element with "The Wandering Islands"; the sexual union is less a union than an act of desperation, an attempt at forgetfulness.

"Under Sedation" is another powerful poem dealing with the nightmare on which our life stands and to which it tries to steel its consciousness. Our sedation is the "drug of custom [that] helps us to adjust." Otherwise "how could we possibly bear / Our civilization for a single day?"[2] Culture is what we use to "keep the heart conditioned not to see" the visions painted by the later Goya: "That old, mad god eating his naked child."

But the attempt to escape from western culture is no real escape— "Gauguin's Menhir, Tahiti" (*LP*, 48) follows the painter in his quest for paradise. In the midst of tropical splendor, however, there stands an "Implacable menhir, alien and alone, / [That] [w]ithdraws into itself, rejects, denies / All this alluring island paradise." It did not take Gauguin long to discover Tahiti was no longer paradise (Hope seems to doubt if it ever had been), that the dead core of life from which he hoped to escape was here as well in the "shuffle of boredom towards the pit of dread." Hope's Gauguin finds that the "eternal honeymoon's improbable lie / Prompted his rage," and, in painting what the "travellers did not wish to see," he "Painted his own predicament most of all." And finally, with his painter's eye he sees through the illusion to the horror of this supposed Eden, that beneath it all was a "volcano god" who "Stood brooding in the dark and nursed his hate."

In a world of such disillusion, of a core that is either emptiness or violence, real human contact is either unattainable or fatal. In "The Coasts

of Cerigo," the deadly Labra "wallows in her bath of time" and her "ladylegs gape darkly as a cave." The very seascape is a lethal sexual lure; the fish swim in and the "love-trap closes on its gullible prey." Human divers on these coasts, whose "brutal masters send them down too deep," will occasionally find a Labra and, throwing away "his knife, his bag of pearl," will wrench her from the ocean; his mates gather round to see the "exquisite, fabled creature as she dies." This meeting is fatal to both: the Labra drowns in air and the diver's lungs are crushed by the pressure at the depths where the Labra lives. The urge of each for the other, their "bodies [that] cling together as they rise," is an embrace of death. The act that might lead to procreation instead leads to extinction; two natures so divided attract as they kill.

Here the vehicle may be the human and the Labra, but clearly the tenor is the human male and female. There is a similar meeting in the first of "Three Romances" (*CP,* 45) that is set on a surreal stage where the persona is to have sex with a woman before an audience and with the accompaniment of an orchestra. (To give a plot summary in cold prose strains credulity; the situation seems somehow believable as it unfolds in the poem.) The speaker is confused and awaits his partner; once she arrives she is seen immediately as a figure of terror who "stalks in her voluptuous rage." The orchestra parallels their lovemaking, the flutes their "long smooth strokes repeat, repeat," and finally "the trumpet shatters all." After the climax comes the humiliation of the male who is left "Like a wet worm upon the boards."

But then he senses the reason for the silence: the very act was death itself and the speaker discovers that the "audience died long ago; / Their bones sit rocking at the show." And then a "you" suddenly appears in the final stanza, the first time the poem, which has clearly displayed an I–it world to this point, ventures into the second person. Perhaps the male can address his partner as "you" rather than "she" now that she, like the audience, is dead?: "Your jaw-bone drops to the parterre."

Is this an instance referred to by Vincent Buckley as being a nihilistic nausea with life itself? Sex is loveless, engenders only death. "Phallus" (*CP,* 30) and "The Elegy" (*CP,* 55) are both primarily exercises in extended metaphor, but in the latter the relation between the lovers is couched in military terms and love is "a romantic slime / That lubricates his way" for the speaker's "huge irrelevance" in the former poem. Certainly the anonymous reviewer in the *Times Literary Supplement* is offended by Hope in this regard: "He sees the skull beneath the skin right enough, but his trouble—and it's his limitation as a poet—is that

he expects us to fall down in astonishment on being told that life is
made up of bones, blood, gristle, guts, and unpalatable, rank juices. He
can't leave it alone. . . . the thing that gets him is that Celia shits. And
the answer to that one is still Lawrence's: how much worse it would be if
she didn't."[3] The first answer to the reviewer would be that, given the
world as it is, yes, it's a good thing that Celia shits. However, that does
not render invalid lamentations about the world being the way it is. But
is the fact that the world is made up of bones, blood, and gristle really
all Hope is addressing? In an essay, "Literature Versus the Universities,"
Hope writes of the plight of the modern writer who works "in an atmosphere of critical inspection equivalent to that of a man trying to make
love under a hundred arc-lights before a large and critical audience. He
may manage to do it, but he will do it as a dramatic performance and
he is much less likely to reach what Donne calls the 'right true end of
love' " (Cave, 169). The "right true end of love," as shall be seen in a
later chapter, is not bounded by the physical; rather, it is rooted in the
material but transcends it, much like the "sensual miracle" described by
Hope in "The Young Girl at the Ball" (CP, 95) whom the speaker
watches and perceives "hidden presences and powers, [is] aware / Of a
promise kept, of mysteries revealed."

Probably the most satisfactory way to refute charges that Hope is
nauseated by the world is to look at his poems of achieved love, which I
shall consider in a later chapter. Hope's poems dealing with physical disgust, violence, and decay are those concerned with incomplete love, love
that is trapped in the physical, where communication between lovers is
impossible, where the act of sexual union is really one of mutual masturbation. That which is merely physical is prey to decay and is destined to
feel the horror of nothingness lurking at its center. In a particularly persuasive and insightful essay, the critic Ross Mezger justifies Hope's use of
the grotesque to "re-focus the reader's attention on the world of reason
and reality." Mezger goes on to discuss the grotesque in a passage vital
enough to cite in its entirety:

> The grotesque in literature consists essentially in the tension between a
> norm or standard, and the exaggeration or distortion of one of its ele-
> ments, usually to an extreme degree. The aberrations or exaggerations
> presented by means of the grotesque initially shock or draw attention to
> themselves. Their further role, however, is to draw the reader's attention,
> by implication, to the norm, standard, attitude or value from which the
> grotesque is a deviation. (270)

The grotesque thus plays a very similar role to satire. There is a fine line between revulsion and rejection; Hope's less-successful poems in this vein tend to wallow in waste rather than by implication affirm the norm from which excess parts. When Hope is not trapped by the darkness of his subject matter, he affirms that the act of kind is antilife if not acted with kindness.

"Three Romances: I" is concerned with love that is essentially pornographic. But Hope is as concerned with repudiation of self-righteous abstention from love as he is with love that is mired in the self, which is pornography or mere self-gratification. In "The Planctus: IX," he retells the story of the Fall in which "Adam, indignant, would not eat with Eve." Eve is driven alone from Paradise, but God supplies her with a mate. Adam, meanwhile, watches them growing old while he remains alone "immortal, young, with virtue crowned, / Sterile and impotent and justified."[4]

Paradise to this Adam would be as flawed as Tahiti to Gauguin. But sterile love rather than abstention is much more dominant in Hope's work: the failure to love while still availing oneself of love's mechanical pleasures. Love in such a context becomes a contest, usually a deadly one. The open warfare between the sexes is even more apparent in "Massacre of the Innocents" (*CP*, 16), which is based on a painting of Cornelis van Haarlem. The scene depicts a group of mothers attempting to protect their babies from Herod's troops. The full anger of the male is bent on the destruction of the feminine; the scene is "the grotesque / Abortion of his love-dream." The act of slaughter becomes a brutal parody of the act of love, and the penis gives way to the knife: "Freckled with blood his knife-arm plunges straight / For the fat suckling's throat" driven onward by "his contraceptive hate." The arm freckled with blood is a masterful touch that makes the knife/penis cliché work; the word "freckle" connotes such a boyish tone that the full sickness of the actions taken here stands out in violent contrast to the right true end of love. "The Walker" (*CP*, 112) is a poem condemning abortion, the life the persona's "coward heart" destroyed.

"The Meeting" (*CP*, 98) and "Totentanz: the Coquette" (*CP*, 101) are both variations on the Death-and-the-Maiden theme. The male in "The Meeting," a poem reminiscent of Browning's "Porphyria's Lover," has wooed the woman; in his desire to utterly possess her heart, he cuts it out of her breast. The murdered woman had desired to love the man, but the relationship remained unconsummated, probably because of the man's inability to love. He finally can possess her when "within his cruel hands, / The murdered heart begins to beat."

This Browningesque situation of failed love turned to violence takes on more mythic dimensions in "Totentanz." Past midnight, a man with "bald skull and a melancholy grin" waits in a woman's bedroom for her return. She arrives, "breathless in the ecstasy of power," and, ignorant of her guest's presence, she undresses before the mirror. But the unknown lover she has attracted is not some "youthful Antony" but one with a "hollow stare, the rigid mask of bone" whose "lattice of a hand / Clips cold on the ripe triumph of her breast." She considers the "challenge of the male" and then turns to him "In sensuous surrender to her death." Yet even in her surrender, she exercises great power over the male—for the contention between the sexes is for power, power over the other whose utter otherness each seeks to possess. Each of the sexes is incomplete in itself; one can reach out for completeness or stab out in an anger fed by lack. The paradox is that while one sex will attempt to find itself fulfilled in the other, the sexes often seem totally foreign to each other, different species with conflicting claims.

"The Double Looking Glass" (CP, 167) further develops themes expressed in "Totentanz" and is one of the most important poems in the Hope canon. The poem retells the story of Susannah and the Elders. It is a highly musical piece written for two voices that weave in and out, Susannah and the Elders, the feminine and the masculine. Having stripped and entered her pool, Susannah senses a foreign presence, but then rationalizes, "My foolish fear refracts a foolish dream." The coquette in "Totentanz" stands before her mirror; Susannah becomes one with it as the pool she enters is both a physical and metaphysical mirror: "Here all things have imagined counterparts." She voices her oneness with Creation, a world from which the male alone is excluded. She is "as all things living," but the male "Cowers from his world in clothes."

Immediately, the male voice enters, harsh, lustful, to speak of her hand that "Plunders the braided treasure of her hair." The verb is violent. The voice rasps out Susannah's name, which sounds to her a "hiss," a "rustle in the sedge . . . fierce susurrus." But again she convinces herself of her privacy: she is in a walled, locked garden that she terms a "private dream." Yet her garden, and by extension she herself, have been trespassed upon already; the dream that holds her is that of the men. If "the nakedness of woman is a pool," each observer will see the reflection of his own wishes. In seeking the other, all that is found is a reflection of the self. The psychic rape of Susannah has already begun.

Following on Susannah's drifting on the "languid current of the day," the masculine voice that enters commenting on the "sunlight sliding on

a breathing flank" seems especially harsh. It becomes clear that rage has coupled with lust in their mirror; she is not only desired, she is hated because she is desired: "Now, now to wreak upon her Promised Land / The vengeance of the dry branch on the bud." Their plenitude is the opposite of hers, a gross reflection of her purity. The erected penis is a "rod of chastisement." Yet her love is essentially narcissistic; her voice holds nearly all that remains of the poem. This monologue is her own fantasy that, I believe, ends in masturbation.

Although she still thinks that the voice she hears is her own imagination distorting natural sounds, she starts to give her fantasy freer reign. She thinks the eyes of the men are merely "glints" but allows her fancy to play, imagining a young, desirable suitor bashfully hiding in her garden. In desperation, he would have sneaked inside the garden only to find that he was "Caught in the ambush of his reckless joy, / Afraid to stir for fear I call." Her exposed position is, she feels, ironically a pose of power.

This is another reminder of the duality of the world. A double looking glass would be one in which the object not only sees its reflection but the reflection sees its object; the other has consciousness and is conscious of being seen. But the one may see something entirely different from what the other sees. When object meets object, a reflection is shattered, often with great violence. What Susannah sees as the world of man is not the world of man presented in the poem.

Susannah reassures herself that "He lives but in my dream" and decides to dream herself in love, that he will "fill / My loins with thunder till the dream be done." Then after a lovely extended metaphor of a sexual voyage, the fluid dream finds the boy basking nude by the pool but despairing of his love while Susannah watches from the wood. The reflections multiply. As she steals up to surprise him in her dream, the old men steal up on her. They reach her, and the masculine voice again is heard invoking a male god: "Ah, God of Israel, even though alone, / We take her with a lover, in the flush / Of her desires."

The reader will have already seen that these two voices are totally ignorant of each other's nature. For the Elders to "take her with a lover" even though she is alone, Susannah would have had to have been masturbating—the only meeting of the masculine and feminine here is physical; the Elders would have been as incapable of entering her thoughts as she would have been capable of entering theirs. Susannah screams, "I am undone! / What beards, what bald heads burst now from the bush!" The bush of course surrounds the pool, but it is obvious that

a pun on pubic hair is also at play here: are they the horror that her sexual being has produced? It is also tempting with an Australian poet to think of bush as referring to the outback; the word has such a definitive meaning in Australia that it is difficult to mention the term without recalling its most common usage. The barbarous reality breaks through to savage the fragile dream, much as the outback haunts the dweller of cities.

The poem is a remarkable work. But why the antagonism between the parties involved? Is the woman merely innocent? Are the men merely jealous? The answer, I think, can be found in an examination of the role of power, the search for control, found in relationships that do not transcend the physical.

After retirement from teaching, Hope wrote *A Midsummer Eve's Dream: Variations on a Theme by William Dunbar*. The book is a long, meandering but fascinating approach to Dunbar's poem "The Tretis of the Tua Mariit Wemen and the Wedo." In the concluding chapter Hope states

> Man prevails and will prevail because he is on the whole bigger and stronger than women and is not handicapped by child-bearing and child-nurture. But woman has two advantages which ... she has only to exploit as thoroughly as men exploit their physical advantages, to match and perhaps conquer the male. One is the strong, ultimately the irresistible magnet of her sexual attraction and attractiveness, the other is the simple physiological fact that she can continue "in the lists of love" longer than he can and that if she presses her advantage she can in the end exhaust and defeat him.[5]

If the relation between the sexes is a war, the sexual turf is where women will prevail. Woman will use her lures to conquer man, but man, grown resentful of losing this battle, brings violence to the sexual relationship to reaffirm his superiority. This violence has filled several of the poems considered in this chapter.

However, there is an analogous female perspective: the woman who stresses her sexual abilities to humble men. Hope sees the women in Dunbar's poem as this type: "For them the male sex is their natural prey, the material of pleasure to be trapped, used, and used up like any other product of the chase" (*Eve*, 262). Hope terms Dunbar's heroines counterparts that will soon be matched by a similar masculine myth, "Don Juan, to whom every woman is *his* natural prey." Hope adds that these "two parties should confront each other as the counterparts they are,

symbols of the naked morality of the satisfaction of sexual appetites raised to an aristocratic principle of rule" (*Eve*, 262). This "naked morality" leads to cannibalistic relationships in which one partner must use the other for his or her own gratification, where sex becomes mutual masturbation and domination becomes a matter of survival.

The *femme fatale*, or the masculine fear of her, appears in many of Hope's poems. In "Dragon Music" (*CP*, 43) a compliment ("No other man makes love like you") causes a psychic split in the man's identity and makes him one of a parade of lovers. In "The Damnation of Byron" (*CP*, 2), Woman gets to wreak her revenge on a Don Juan who, in the "Hell of Women," merely "seeks companions: but they only bring / Wet kisses and voluptuous legs agape." He has become a "symbol of the male" and finally suffers the "immense derision of Hell." The images develop to a greater and greater engulfment of the male consumed by the female principle.

The sexual battlefield takes over the nursery tale in "Coup de Grâce" (*CP*, 166). Little Red Riding Hood is greeted by the Wolf with his "slavering grin." He seems fearsome, but Little Red Riding Hood is not bothered. Her mouth, which is described in sexual terms ("Velvet red of the rose / Framing each little milk-tooth, / Pink tongue peeping between"), becomes her weapon of defense; she swallows the "Wolf in a trice" and then "Bows, all sugar and spice. / O, what a lady-like trick!" Her mouth resembles the female sexual organs just as the male became a "rod of chastisement" in "The Double Looking Glass."

These two poems, reflections in their own right, were written about the same time and follow each other in the *Collected Poems 1930–1965.* Writing of Hope's work, Geoffrey Hartmann commented: "The power to respond to and suffer the condition of sexual love is the ever-recurring last judgment, the one truly martial test of man" (757). The lovers we have seen are judged harshly because they have found sexual love merely a battleground, an activity in which they can assert their power over their partners.

Oftentimes the nature of reality is such that an act of creation can have unforeseen results. In one of Hope's most famous poems, "Imperial Adam" (*CP*, 83), God presents Adam with Eve. There is something slightly suspicious about her from the beginning; she is termed an "allegory of sense unsatisfied" and her movement makes the appearance of Satan unnecessary: "Sly as the snake she loosed her sinuous thighs." In the act of sexual union, she takes control of Eden; at the moment of orgasm she emits a "terrible and triumphant female cry." This is a love

unlike those considered earlier in this chapter that could not give birth. Here creation itself brings destruction; their baby is the "first murderer." It was this poem that prompted James McAuley to term Hope an atheist Manichee; perhaps a more moderate reading of the poem would reveal not a world divided between the two forces of good and evil, but rather a world in which these forces become intertwined one with the other.

"Imperial Adam" elicits far more questions than it answers. Kevin Hart mentions that Hope intended the poem as a "satire of the medieval theology . . . which presents Eve as a temptress and sex as inherently sinful" but remarks that the "poem exceeds its intention and gets caught up in what it satirises," that the poem "ends up strengthening a myth about women it sets out to ironise" (80). And this raises questions about Hope's work beyond "Imperial Adam." To what extent is his work misogynistic?

Certainly in most of the poems cited in this chapter women do not fare well. But neither do men. Hope is in no danger of being guilty of a trendy political correctness, but there are troubling instances in his work where woman is portrayed as object. Some stanzas of the generally delightful "Six Songs for Chloë" (NP, 33) would not please feminists, and asides such as "skirts fly, showing / Essential girl" ("A Windy Afternoon," LP, 18) may not be found endearing by many. "The Countess of Pembroke's Dream" (LP, 30) is at times close to pornography with its elements of bestiality but is a serious, even subtle, poem. A couple examples in Hope's collection, Orpheus, published when the poet was 84, are also troubling. "Teaser Rams,"[6] except for its prosodic skill, would not seem out of place in a collection of pornography. In "Intimations of Mortality" (O, 15), the speaker calls on the four gospel writers to "keep the wicked whores away" but then reconsiders—"I'd like some snatch before I die." And there are other examples to be found.

Part of the unseemliness may be based unfairly in the knowledge that some of these poems were written by an old man, but I think the worst are failures of judgment rather than symptoms of a core misogyny in Hope's work. He is one of the major poetic explorers of sexuality in the English language, perhaps the most important one from a male perspective. It is treacherous turf. The sexual act can easily become brutal and coercive; although it may spring from a mutually subjective love, it objectifies its desires onto the other. For the male, at least, sex is an aggressive act, even though it may spring from the greatest tenderness. Because it may bring great joy it is also fraught with danger; it can be

both unifying and divisive. Hope has explored this turf bravely, and I find it forgivable when he occasionally stumbles.

Indeed, Kevin Hart finds a "thread of feminism which runs throughout [Hope's] poems and criticism" that "recommends a change in social attitude, not structure" (102). In the ironically titled "Advice to Young Ladies" (*CP,* 207), Hope writes of the fate of the vestal virgin Postumia who managed to avoid execution but survives with a crushed spirit. In the same piece, he also mentions women "who found that the disgrace / Of being a woman made genius a crime." He ends by asking if perhaps a major reason for the fall of empires has been that they "Trusted the servile womb to breed free men?" The poem "Botany Bay or The Rights of Woman,"[7] in which the heroine reforms both her place in society and her criminal husband, is another example of a work that could not have been written by a woman hater. Hope works in dualities, and the recognition and exploration of the male and female dialectic is one central to his opus.

This double nature of the world that manifests itself in love is also evident in art. Hope has always held the viewpoint that sex and art are mirror images. He of course is not alone in thinking this: Claude Rawson points out that "Analogies between poetic and sexual potency were not unusual in early modernist masters."[8] This was certainly the case with Yeats, as it was from early youth with Hope; when he was 14 he wrote a poem linking sex with poetry and comments on the experience many years later: "This is the first time, I remember, that I was aware of the strong connection between sexual feeling—love if you like, they were not divided in my mind at the time, nor indeed since—and the impulse to poetry. It was a feeling that later on led me to remark in a still unpublished poem: 'The poet's, in a certain sense, / Male organ to the human mind.' A view I still hold" (*NC,* 8). And this is not the case of a writer as critic claiming one thing and as poet doing another. Chris Wallace-Crabbe says of Hope that "he tends to present art and love as analogically parallel"[9], and we shall see many examples of this in upcoming chapters.

One would expect to find in art, then, some of the same dangers one finds in love: the miracle of creation containing within it the seed of death. The muse, in the poem of the same name (*CP,* 48), is compared to Arachne, among others; she has a "ferocious purpose in the night" and "hangs / In loveliness no wisdom could invent / And conscious of the poison in her fangs." This poem was written in response to James

McAuley's poem that portrayed the muse in more conventional and complimentary terms.

Probably the finest example of the lethal side of art can be found in "Moschus Moschiferous" (*NP,* 10), a poem William Jay Smith claims to be "one of the truly great poems of the century."[10] It is a brilliant work, and brilliantly understated. The poem, written for St. Cecilia's Day, is termed a song, St. Cecilia being the patron saint of music. The verses describe in a matter-of-fact way how the Kastura deer are slaughtered in Tibet for their musk pods and are in danger of becoming extinct. The Kastura deer hunt is additionally cruel in its method of luring the deer to their death. The animals are brought out of hiding by the music of a flute: "the bowstrings snap / And poisoned shafts bite sharp into the kill."

Here is a modern parallel to the unicorn. It is a gift of art, of joy, that brings death, as Adam and Eve's joy brought Cain. But the greatness of the poem rests in the final stanza, a quatrain so understated as to almost obscure its teeth: Hope addresses "Divine Cecilia" and the mysterious power of music and closes "In honour of your day / Accept this song I too have made for you." Is this also a song that somehow brings death while being concerned with the lethal power of music? The offering of the poem to Cecilia seems a threat, considering the subject matter of the song. The conclusion is as enigmatic as the theme. The matter of fact-ness of the tone is perfectly modulated. Many of the poems considered in this chapter suffer from overstatement. In "Moschus Moschiferous" Hope is at his masterly best.

Judith Wright claims that Hope is "torn between a loathed reality and a vision of eternal meaning" (190). We have seen the presence of death in the sheer physicality of life, in sex, and now even in art. Vincent Buckley, as usual, is perceptive in commenting that Hope's "advanced tactile sense gives him an unusually, almost an abnormally, acute sense of the physical—of its contours and its relations, even of the feel of its inner biological life. And he is quite as conscious of decomposition and distortion as he is of the positive *being* which it contains" (154). But can one base artistic work on this decomposition and distortion, or is this merely an aberration with Hope that readers must overlook and thus turn to his other poems? Instead, I think this is the base from which Hope begins, his own "foul rag-and-bone shop of the heart." It is from such a basis, from roots firmly anchored in physical reality, that Hope builds his transcendental vision. Chris Wallace-Crabbe notes that Hope's "concern for lucid heights stems from a contemplation of murky

depths; the shapely fountain rises not in spite of but because it has its source in the chasm where the chartless waters of the unconscious run" (396).

In his "Sonnets to Baudelaire" (*NP,* 25) Hope pays tribute to and holds discussion with a poet he thinks a kindred spirit. Hope writes that Baudelaire "tilled our rotting paradise" and from it "Raised monstrous blooms and taught my tongue the craft." He states that "few around us know they walk in hell"; the artist should deal with the reality that "the universe / Expands, but something's slimy underfoot." One of the roles of the artist is to "in the womb say to each unborn lover: / The hand that rocks the cradle rules the grave."

Yet though the physical must be transcended, it is the material through which we reach the spiritual. In another of the Baudelaire sonnets, Hope states that the metaphor for the poem is "two lovers in a bed" who become "one body, one motion and one breath" and "every simile [is] an act of love." Here is union and transcendence firmly rooted in the physical, but in the physical viewed aright. Except for this mystical enhancement of the flesh, the flesh, in itself, is a trap. And this is driven home by the more successful of the poems considered in this chapter. Ross Mezger comments that "Hope is aware of the grotesque as a major poetic technique, which not only presents the ambiguity and duality of existence, but also is a means towards restoring the reader's faith in the world of reason" (283). Well aware by this point of the fact that "something's slimy underfoot," we must now turn to consider how "the universe / Expands." To create a transcendent art from physical decay is indeed a heroic act, and it is to Hope's use of the heroic that we must now turn our attention.

Chapter Four

The Heroic:
The Argument of Arms

When the heroic appears in most twentieth-century literature, it is usually presented ironically; the unheroic nature of the present is clearly displayed by its comparison to the grander standards of past ages. Such heroic juxtaposition was a frequently used tool of the moderns, Eliot's "The Love Song of J. Alfred Prufrock" being one of the best-known examples.

One of Hope's uses of the heroic is just such a juxtaposition to show the bankruptcy of the contemporary scene. I have already examined some examples in his work, in particular "Conquistador" and "The Kings." In "The Sacred Way" (*LP,* 22) what the reader finds is not so much a comparison as a lament; the contemporary is made smaller not as much by contrast with the heroic as by the absence of anything to compare. The speaker wakes in the night and considers the present age and wonders what heroes, what images it has to sustain the imagination. He then acknowledges that the world he "grew up in now belongs to the past" and mentions several heroes progressing from classical (Hercules) to biblical (Samson) to medieval legend (Roland and Robin Hood) and comments "We were fortunate indeed."

Like Yeats, Hope compared the past of his own family favorably to the mundane present. "Morning Meditation" (*CP,* 205) begins with the speaker before his mirror shaving, suppressing "the natural man." He thinks back to his bearded grandfather who even in his old age, "if a wench appeared . . . catch and cuddle her tight." His father shaved— "He did it to pleasure his wife"—and "in his sixtieth year" rejected the decline into old age and "Picked up the blade once more, / And cut his throat to the bone." The speaker, however, keeps "the beast at bay / With a safety razor," and is altogether a more timorous creature who lives "by the Golden Rule"; this relative timidity brings about a self-loathing when he thinks of his father and grandfather, "that sinful pair / And curse myself for a fool."

Such a family tree does not really exist for Hope: the characters bear little relation to the actual members of the Hope clan. The sensitive reader would suspect that the poem is not autobiographical because of the tone, but its fiction does not harm the poem as a work of art. Nevertheless, the fact that "Morning Meditation" is purely fictional means family traditions are not a fertile link to the heroic for Hope; Yeats, for all his exaggerations, did have ancestors whose feats lent themselves to poetic embellishment. Hope, on the other hand, almost never mentions his father or mother in his poetry.

Hope, therefore, seeks access to the heroic past through his readings of history and art. Chris Wallace-Crabbe noted the heroic stature of many of Hope's characters: "There is something operatic about the way his more-than-life-size figures sing out their arias against exotic backdrops. Defiant energy rather than delicate perception is commonly the distinguishing mark" (398). Again, comparison with Byron offers illumination. For all Hope's critical claims for satire and the discursive mode, he once again resembles more the Byron of *Manfred* than of *Don Juan*. This defiant energy comes from an assertion of the will against insuperable odds, a Nietzschean will to power. The hero is heroic because he stares doom in the face; his is an affirmation of the will that affirms at the same time it realizes it is doomed by the sheer facts of existence.

The structure of "The Pleasure of Princes" (*CP*, 64) is among the most straightforward of Hope's poems. The work begins "What pleasures have great princes?" and immediately answers "These: to. . . ." The rest of the poem is a catalogue of the supposed pleasures. The pleasures, if pleasures they are, lie in the daily contemplation and use of power, bringing down families and ravaging cities. Their pleasure cannot only be found in war and vengeance but in manipulation: they are able to "engage / The cunning of able, treacherous ministers / To serve, despite themselves, the cause they hate." In short, he sounds like an altogether unpleasant character. What is praised here is not so much the end that might be reached as control of the means; it is in the use of power for its own sake that the pleasure of statecraft lies. This is still the struggle for control that was examined in the previous chapter, but now in the realm of politics rather than in the sexual domain.

The last and greatest pleasure of power for Hope's prince is overcoming, though but for a time, the opposition of existence. Now old and having begotten "worthless sons," the ruler can "By starlight climb the battlements" whereon he will watch over the city and think "my great

demon grumbles in his sleep / And dreams of his destruction, and of mine.' " The "great demon" resembles the volcano god of "Gauguin's Menhir, Tahiti," but the ruler has not fallen to the *ennui* that has infected the islanders. Even in his old age, he is defiant, hardier than the moving sentry who "hugs himself for cold" on his more prosaic night watch and muses on destruction with a smile. Though the great demon may gnaw as relentlessly as the snake at the roots of Yggdrasil, the will of the prince is unbroken though trapped in dying flesh.

According to the classical ethos, to control one's destiny one had to will one's end. After reaching the summit, the only direction in which one can move is downward. Life is not static; one moment is best because all other moments are worse. "The Trophy" (*CP,* 68) asserts that "In the instant of success" one senses the shadow of failure, that the greatest of triumphs still cannot sustain the hero long in the chill airs of utter success. To avoid being undone by fate, one must undo one's fate.

The artist—building is often a metaphor for art in Hope—and the lover are supplied a symbol from the very insufficiency of their art or love: the "Roman soldier" is referred to as "Image both of love and art." This leader exerted his "great captain's rigid will" and drove his troops to victory even though outnumbered. But at the height of his success, "when the campaign was won / By the single force of pride," the conquering hero "Heard the ghost within him groan" and committed suicide. The great man shapes the defeated rabble into victory and then refuses to wait while fate works its will with him. Of course, one might respond that suicide grants the ghost within an immediate victory rather than a slower one, but this is not a poem espousing suicide, though one is tempted to admire the resolve if not the judgment of both the Roman soldier and Hope's mythical father of "Morning Meditation." "The Trophy" seems more of a rhetorical gesture than a directive, a posture rather than a position.

Greater clarity is offered in what seems at first glance quite a contrasting poem to "The Trophy." "Antechinus" (*Ant,* 18) concerns itself with the rodent of the same name, a marsupial about the size of the mouse. The poem begins with a classical (via Shakespeare) salutation that at first seems a case of heroic juxtaposition at its most extreme: "Antechinus, my hero, small furred friend, / I come to bury, not praise you. . . ." But as the poem develops, it becomes clear that Hope is concerned with something much more intricate than it first appears.

The male antechinus is born in September and leaves the pouch in November or December. He lives a solitary life, if he can keep from

being eaten, until he develops in June and July an antagonism toward any other antechini he might meet. In late August, the antechinus takes a mate. The female is usually unwilling and has to be raped. Mating can be violent—the female has sometimes been fatally injured—and will last anywhere between 5 and 12 hours. Shortly after his lengthy and only bout of sex, the male dies.

Although the mating results in death, Hope wonders whether the height of passion somehow gives mere existence a focus, if sex, "that supreme delirium" manages to redeem "this short, savage irony, your life?" For if the sexual act contains the doom of the male, the coupling begins to take on dimensions of the heroic, even considering the ingloriousness of the beast; by contrast, the human's choice is not nearly as heroic as the rodent's in that it consists of "love repeated to fritter itself away / In change and failure or final sad decay." The human fate is, by and large, a much more comfortable one than that of antechinus, but oddly less noble. The heroic disappears from love when death disappears; perhaps only that which is lethal can be felt fully.

Hope goes on to such a consideration and wonders whether he would have been capable of the heroic action if his "naked Venus beckoned, with her full / Breasts and bold thighs and, on her neck, a skull?" To have been faced with such a situation would have at least one redeeming aspect—love might be something known solely in an unalloyed state, not frittered away in failure as it now too often is. The speaker is forced to admit that this is mere speculation, that we must "accept our lot and live," but still the question must linger: how is the heroic act possible without the presence of the lethal threat? And is the unheroic somehow a cheat, life not lived at its height, the withered herb of joy of "The Lingam and the Yoni"?

We have already seen in "The Pleasure of Princes" that the unsurrendering will that affirms its own power in the face of defeat partakes of the heroic and that, to the unbending will, life itself is a lethal threat. Any human power is an assertion of worth and by nature aristocratic, much as satire is aristocratic in telling people what they should or should not value. Any creation is an act of will and an assertion of power. If art is to be heroic, it must be concerned with power; art is an assertion and as such is an act of defiance, to time if nothing else. Such a view of poetry is the primary concern of Hope's essay "The Argument of Arms" from *The Cave and the Spring*.

The central works under consideration in this essay are Marlowe's *Tamburlaine* dramas. Hope says that this most unlikable hero for whom

the plays are named "has the natural genius for power and he actually tests it against all possible contenders." Perfection is the end of striving, and Tamburlaine "achieves the perfection of human nature in a world in which only one man can be perfect. This standard of values means that the man who imposes his will on all others is, in a sense, the only fully human being among them. For he alone has achieved the full possibilities of the human. He subsumes all values into himself. It means in fact that the man who can achieve this and maintain his position must have gifts and qualities above the human. He partakes of the divine" (120). As appalling as such a doctrine may be, within the bounds of the world described in the play, this position is the only one that has anything more than a tangential validity. The world of the dramas is a continual battleground; the great man is the supreme warrior. Hope himself postulates the necessity for such a narrow world for Marlowe's argument when Hope writes of the scene in which the generals plead that Tamburlaine be spared because "if he perishes then all is meaningless. If there is no morality, no beauty, no value but in absolute and supreme power, then the tragedy of Tamburlaine is the tragedy of man himself" (127). The conditionality of the last sentence is important. If the world is to be defined in this way, Tamburlaine does "partake of the divine."

But in the same manner I can construct a trivialized argument in which if all meaning exists in a particular tree, the toppling of that tree would necessarily lead to nihilism. However, a finding predicated on such terms can easily be avoided by altering the premises. If all meaning exists in A, then anything non-A is meaningless. But there is no need to subscribe to such flimsy premises. One can as easily reject the argument that has been advanced so far for Tamburlaine. But then Hope alters the argument in quite an extraordinary way:

> If Tamburlaine were merely a supreme military genius, the argument which asserts his total superiority and perfection would be unconvincing. But Tamburlaine is a poet. He conceives poetry as concentrating in its highest conceivable form, the whole of beauty, imagination and music into 'one poem's period', just as he concentrates all power in himself. . . . Power is his medium, as power is his nature and his genius. Poetry shares the supremacy of nature, for it is the natural language of beauty, of intellect and of power, the three perfect things. . . . poetry accepts only success, and grants lasting life only to absolute success. It recognizes no gradations and no second best. (127–28)

Hope then quotes Hazlitt on Coriolanus in a passage concerned with the relationship between the language of poetry and the language of power. Hazlitt describes the poetic imagination as an "exaggerating and exclusive faculty" that "takes from one thing to add to another." This imagination is contrasted with the understanding Hazlitt terms a "dividing and measuring faculty" that judges things "according to their relations to one another." Whereas the imagination is a "monopolizing faculty," which "seeks the greatest quantity of present excitement by inequality and disproportion," the understanding is a "distributive faculty which seeks the greatest quantity of ultimate good" through the processes of "justice and proportion." Poetry is aristocratic, existing by contrast and admitting "of no medium." Hazlitt concludes by stating that poetry "puts the individual for the species, the one above the infinite many, might before right."[1]

Thus reinforced by Hazlitt, Hope concludes his essay in grand style: "Those who wish to understand *Tamburlaine* should read and re-read this passage [from Hazlitt] for it represents the Argument of Arms translated into the Argument of Poetry. And those who wish to understand the real nature of poetry would do well to have *Tamburlaine* by heart, for the heart of the matter is that the Argument of Arms and the Argument of Poetry are in their essence the same" (128). Hope contends that the language of poetry is aristocratic, at least in its relation to other uses of language. And it is true that the language of poetry is always different from that of speech, even when it stresses its roots in everyday speech. It is also different in degree if not in kind from the language of prose. The line takes precedence over the sentence, that solid foot soldier of ordinary communication. To recognize this difference is not necessarily an argument for the supremacy of poetry, though it can be the basic supposition of such an argument.

It is not much of a step from this point to a consideration of poetry as the natural language of beauty. Indeed, such a statement seems almost a cliché, even to people who never read poetry. Such a belief would not seem odd to the average businessperson, who might often associate beauty with uselessness, but the accompanying claim that poetry is also the language of power would seem most bizarre.

We must first come to some understanding of what exactly is meant by power. Certainly the prose of the Pentagon is about as far removed as language can be from poetry. Power is used in this discussion of poetry in a heroic rather than a bureaucratic sense. The great epics are written

in verse. *Paradise Lost* or *The Divine Comedy* is impossible to conceive of in prose. One needs the grander resources of the language that are more readily available to the poet than to the prose writer for the cosmic vision of a Dante or a Milton. Poetry, for Hope, is the supreme organizing principle of existence. As Kevin Hart rightly claims, "All true art for Hope, whether epic or lyric, is monumental in its essence; it consumes the artist and entombs him, thereby raising him to the status of a king or god" (69).

A lifelong project of Hope's has been an attempt to purge and amend the text of Marlowe's *Doctor Faustus*. No original manuscript of the play exists, and the texts that have come down to us have been altered substantially. While Hope freely admits that much guesswork is involved, he has struck what he deems as obviously not Marlowe from the play and rewritten various passages in a way he believes to be more consistent with the playwright's work. In his reworking of the first scene of Act II, Hope gives a speech to Wrath during the procession of the Seven Deadly Sins in which Wrath claims to be "source and fountain-head of strife / And root of war" but then makes the larger claim that "strife alone maintains the frame of things." If strife is central to creation, then "the man of wrath, the conqueror / [will be he] Who understands the argument of arms." This man has the right—because he has the power—to "trample in the blood of slaughter'd men, / Treading upon the necks of captive kings, / Pursuing the conquer'd with insatiate rage" and "is the man of men *par excellence* / As nature's paragon and masterpiece."[2]

Although the dominant metaphor here is still militaristic, it is couched in much broader implications. Certainly we have already seen in the preceding chapter how "Even in our elements do we contend." The physical realm is one of constant warfare; the flesh wages war on itself as surely as does one species on another. The male and female are in conflict. From this strife comes "order, justice, beauty, polity." The tension of oppositions is creative: "strife alone maintains the frame of things." This is even a scientific principle; an object keeps its shape only if the pressure exerting its force is equal both inside and outside the object. Otherwise the object collapses or explodes.

The difficulty with this entire analogy is that its tenor works but its vehicle does not. The nature of war has been drastically altered; human nature has not changed. The world can be destroyed not through heroic acts but with the pushing of a button. Although the metaphor is grounded in the military, the argument of arms is as out of place there as

it is in the artistic sphere; the grounded metaphor is out of harmony with itself.

To use such a conceit requires rhetorical flourishes that veil the essential weakness of the unifying metaphor. This becomes evident in "Invocation" (*CP*, 65), which begins with a quote from Heraclitus, to whom reference was also made in the Wrath's speech from *Faustus*: "To the gods all things are fair and good and right, but men hold some things wrong and some right." It is not long before one senses the ghost of Heraclitus being shouldered aside by that of Nietzsche. The speaker, obviously a poet, offers a Faustian invocation that could as easily be an invocation of Mephistopheles as of the muse. The speaker, in his fortieth year, is still uncertain of the purpose that draws him, though he has, over the years, made some progress. Yet he finds he lacks the courage of his convictions, missing "the habit of courage that should be mine" through which he would "Engender power and beauty on our night."

The rhetoric here grows more Mephistophelean; what gives the powerful the courage to light the common way leads to their damnation. When the persona seeks to bring himself to the fore as more than a mere supplicant, the rhetoric becomes unacceptably heavy-handed when he refers to the Immortals: "That breed is in my bones." This is followed by questions that lead even deeper into hubris, seeming more and more out of proportion to the issues involved: "My passion, my gift, my vision can I betray? / Must for my pride the innocent be undone?" This currency seems greatly inflated indeed. Such rhetoric could work were it put into the mouth of a historical personage. Yet, as it is, the temptation is too great to see the speaker as the poet before a self-inflating mirror. Yes, I think "that breed" may be in Hope's bones, no matter how unbecoming it may sound as self-election.

But how will the "innocent be undone" from his pride? This is certainly overkill invited by the inapplicability of the argument of arms to aesthetic concerns. Richard III's offer to trade his kingdom for a horse may have been a desperate gesture, but there is still something of the heroic about it: the stakes are high and the danger is immediate. And he does have a kingdom to trade. A poet, in Richard's situation, pleading for a pen, suggests a diminution; the vocation of the poet may be more noble than that of a king, but it is also of necessity a very different sort of calling. When Shelley spoke of the poet as the unacknowledged legislator of the world, he did not in any way mean to suggest that the poet should write amendments rather than verse. The decisions of the poet are of a different nature from that of the person in power, though they

may share similar concerns. Poetry that resembles a civics lesson is a diminution of poetry.

The speaker in "Invocation" is trapped between the dualism of the dragon and the lion. The dragon is custom, but the lion "guards the eternal measures of the world." This lion in no way honors the frail human standards by which most men live: "at the laws of men her lip is curled." Now it may be true that a vision is that which "crowns the might of [the poet's] desire"—it certainly was the case with Yeats. But the conceit is carried too far; one can almost see the poet approach his study in full armor, lance in hand.

"Pyramis or The House of Ascent" (*CP*, 67) suffers from similar problems. The poem first seems to honor the sheer assertion of the will in which "a nation piling stones / Under the lash in fear, in sweat, in haste" becomes the emblem of those who construct "To outlast time, spend life to house old bones." Yet the despotic nature of the enterprise is glossed over in Hope's glorification of the resolved will. He writes of these pharaohs as "Taking, like genius, their prerogative / Of blood, mind, treasure." It is here that one can see the essential difference between the pharaoh and the artist. When the artist asserts his or her will, the consequences are very different from those that result when a political leader chooses to exert power. It is hard to think of a creative genius who was as unbending to conventional morality as Wagner, yet Wagner's "sins" are petty compared to those of Hitler, whose prerogatives are of an entirely different order. Yet Hope has his Pharaoh speak the Argument of Arms: " 'If you lack slaves, make war! The measure of things / Is man, and I of men.' "

This hymn to power does not end with the human realm; G. A. Wilkes indicates the source of the poem: " 'Pyramis' was suggested by one of the theories presented in I. E .S. Edwards's *The Pyramids of Egypt,* that the Pharaohs built the pyramids as a stairway to heaven, challenging the gods."[3] Indeed, the poem states that the "gods themselves unwilling await him still / And must be overcome." (One is reminded of the Tower of Babel, an edifice that resulted in a confusion of tongues rather than a triumph of speech.) However, once temporal power has been elevated to the point where it is ready to duel with the gods, then the transition to consideration of the artist is difficult to resist; the artist is, after all, godlike in the ability to create. "I think of other pyramids, not in stone": rather, he is thinking of the "great, incredible monuments of art."

The poet then invokes Blake, Milton, and Swift as "builders of the pyramid everywhere!" Yet the heroic indifference of the artist includes

an indifference to the dragon of custom, and custom would include the pharaoh; the artistic assertion of the will requires, paradoxically, an indifference to the powers of this world that pose such a threat to the artist. Hope himself in his essay "The Activists" (*Cave*, 29) warns against the chilling effect the temporal state has on the artist who condescends to serve it.

It is one thing to say that Blake, Milton, and Swift were unbending in the face of those forces that, while they make life comfortable, are a bane to creation. It is quite another to relate their artistic courage to the political obsessions of a despot. In *A Late Picking* Hope wrote a poem honoring a Jewish poet killed by the Nazis, "In Memoriam: Gertrud Kolmar, 1943" (84), and Hope has consistently spoken against political oppression. Yet if there ever were a twentieth-century pyramid builder it would have to be Adolph Hitler. It is true that art is not democratic; talent forms an aristocracy and is not fairly divided among various groups in a diverse society. But this is not to say that art is antidemocratic, a mistake made by too many of the modernists. The artist may be different from the average person—but that doesn't mean that the artist is a better person. Indeed, all too often this is patently not the case.

Hope is more successful when he links the heroic and the artistic through their meeting ground of love. The previous chapter demonstrated how sex can be a battlefield, a competition for power. However, in the poem "The Lamp and the Jar" (*CP*, 79), Hope is able to illustrate more happily the union of the sexes.

The structure of the poem is obvious. It is a work of resolved dualities: the lamp and the jar, the "you" and the "I," the two verses of the poem. The woman, addressed in the second person, is a "vessel full of holy oil" that fills the "pure flanks of the containing stone." The woman is the "source alone" that "Distils those fruitful tears the Muses weep." Once again woman is the other, but she is no longer terrifying or despised.

The speaker next identifies himself as "the lamp before the sacred ark" who draws "from your loins this inexhaustible joy." The meeting here is one of opposites in accord; the poem never discusses what the jar gains from the lamp—the first-person viewpoint is decidedly male—but it is clear that what is being described is not rape. The poem closes with the language of power, but not the power of Tamburlaine—this king is himself transformed by the encounter as the speaker sees an "unknown king, with my transfigured face, / {who} Bends your immortal body to his delight." The female being is at least godlike if not a god. Yet the

king has had to build no pyramid to achieve this union. "The Lamp and the Jar" is not one of Hope's best poems—lines such as "The shapes of terror and inhuman woe" do not help matters—but it softens the language of power through the introduction of the feminine as man's complement rather than his foe, a conquering of the other giving way to a mutual exploration.

The poem "Parabola" (*LP,* 46) is an even better example of a heroic motif in Hope handled with a restraint not evident when the poet deals with the Argument of Arms unalloyed by the presence of the feminine. The first two verses introduce the main metaphor of the piece, how the princess lies in a trance for a hundred years, enchanted in a castle guarded by a jungle of briars that contains the "Bones of the youths who sought her." Much as the Golden Bough and Aeneas, the obstacle can be conquered only by the chosen: the thorns will give access only to the one "whom alone Fortune reserves the prize."

After waking the maiden with a kiss, the knight "ravishes her century of sleep." What lifts "Parabola" from the ordinary is Hope's daring leap from the fairy tale to the scientific; biology reenacts the poem's action in microcosm. Another princess waits "in her womb" and is being sought by the male sperm, personified as a "horde of lovers" who burst "between the gates, / All doomed but one."

The following three verses are flawed by too ponderous moralizing as to how we are a composite of biological necessity and free will, but they assert that the "life of Nature is a formal dance" in which the "marriage of linked cause and random chance / Gives birth perpetually to the unforeseen." The world has gone from being a battlefield to being a formal dance; a dance, of course, requires a partner. So does a battle, but a dance implies harmony, a working together, and usually entails both the male and female principles. The world is seen less as something to conquer than as something to explore. The assertion of the will for both the artist and the scientist is an act of fearless exploration, a seducing of the world to reveal its secrets; the speaker, like the knight, must meet his challenge.

Despite the cavalier closing of "Oh well, here goes!" it should be evident that the spirit of "Parabola" is nearly the antithesis of that of a poem such as "Pyramis." It is the difference between seduction and rape, celebrating the workings of nature and human nature far more positively than "Antechinus." "Parabola," despite its flaws as a poem, evidences a maturing vision in Hope of the power of the artist, a power essentially different from that found on the battlefield. How much more

achieved is the honor accorded the Icelandic scholar, Ian Maxwell: "The man of action in the scholar's chair, / Like Gunnar gentle and like Ari wise" (*Ant,* 85). Gentleness and intellect are not the hallmarks of the pharaoh.

Vivian Smith wrote that for Hope "Creative achievement, effort of will, is seen as one of the ways out of the dilemma of human isolation in a world without religious belief" (377). I have attempted to demonstrate how the Argument of Arms is incompatible with the Argument of Art, but one more point of discrimination must be drawn. In Hope's canon, there is usually a clear distinction between the heroic and the mythic. The heroic is human assertion of will against the world, an attempt to overcome by force that which separates the human from the divine. The mythic is more subtle and implies a transformation of the world; the familiar is given meaning because it can partake of the universal. Art does not create a different world by destroying physical reality. Art transforms, translates, or transcreates the existing world in ways that endow it with meaning. Meaning comes not through conquering but through understanding. Such is the distinction between the heroic and the mythic.

If there is one ghost that has hung over this chapter, it is that of Yeats. Yeats was absorbed by the heroic and the mythic—"Easter 1916" can in part be read as a debate between these two forces—and he is himself probably the quintessential example of the individual forging himself into greatness. In the late 1940s when Hope was writing most of his poems that deal with the Argument of Arms, he also wrote a very curious poem, "William Butler Yeats" (*CP,* 72). The first four stanzas are a well-done tribute, with little of the unexpected. Yeats "found at last that noble, candid speech" and is himself something of a hero: he was "afraid neither of lust nor hate" and "is compared to Swift and Blake." The cited poets, sans Milton, are the same as those named in "Pyramis."

But then Hope does something quite extraordinary, something that may harm the unity of the poem but that lifts it well out of the realm of the ordinary tribute. He concludes the poem with two verses that seem a significant departure from those that preceded them. After describing a night of love, Hope says "order and content / Closed the Platonic Year" and wonders what led the lovers to look in the "glass of the Great Memory," recognizing themselves as "the eternal moments, in your book, / That we had grown to be"? Chris Wallace-Crabbe, who terms these stanzas an "astonishing tangent from all that has gone before," offers the following possible explanation, one that deserves to be cited at length:

That Platonic Year is presumably only a figurative bit of play with Yeats's materials. But what is the status of his book, his poetry? At a simple level the lines tell us that lovers go to Yeats's poems and recognize themselves there. But the book is also 'the glass of the Great Memory' and their recognitions are also 'eternal moments'. The poetry of Yeats becomes another consummation, over and above the all-night blessing of the lovers; both love and art offer an ascent into the Great Memory, the *Anima Mundi,* but it is the work of a poet which can provide identification for lovers, showing them, figured in the artifice of eternity, what they have grown to be. (399–400)

There is something beyond chance that led the lovers to the recognition of what they have become through the dual creative acts of love and art. The Yeats in the first four stanzas could have been simply a satirist; what is most clearly shown is the poet's uncompromising scorn of the follies of this world. What is found in the concluding stanzas is the world transformed. Anger has given way to love, and it is love and art that have transformed both the lovers and the world. The former attitude, the anger at the world and the waging of war with it, is typical of the heroic as it appears in Hope's work. But what we find at the end of the poem is the world transformed, the realm of the mythic, a world where the Argument of Arms is an idle posture.

Chapter Five
The Mythic: Night

Only one Tamburlaine can exist at any time; the hero is the greatest of men, all others, by his scale, being failures. The heroic is perhaps the most individualistic of creeds. The mythic, on the other hand, fosters a sense of community; the individual existence is given validity because it partakes of a higher reality, because it is not unique. The gods are not to be conquered; rather, mythology is in many ways a record of commerce between the temporal and the divine.

For myth to have continuing meaning for humanity in a scientific age, it must not be static. Myth has validity because new myths are continually being reshaped in ways that speak to the contemporary predicament. Most modern myths have narrowed to some extent, the cosmological having given way to the nationalistic. Almost our only grand myths remaining are those of science—a topic for the next chapter.

Hope has frequently transformed the familiar myths. David Kalstone has written of Hope: "His skill is partly one of reinterpretation. The literary scene is one we know, but the characters have been assigned new positions on stage."[1] In "The End of a Journey" (*CP,* 1) Ulysses has come back to Ithaca, but finds his triumphant return to a life of peace, a life of administration rather than heroism, hollow. Although the poem covers ground usurped by Tennyson, Hope's is still a fine treatment of the theme. Arising in the morning and going down to the beach, Ulysses watches "his enemy the sea" and dismisses "the petty kingdom he called home," and prays to Athena while knowing full well she will not come. What does come to him from deep within his memory is the Sirens' transformed song that ends terming Ulysses in Ithaca as a "castaway upon so cruel a shore."

Ithaca becomes the hero's worst banishment. It is worth noting that Hope began this poem at about the time he worked on the first drafts of "Australia." Just having returned home from England, Hope found in Ulysses a personal myth. "The End of a Journey," while denying homecoming in the truest sense, affirms the sense of striving that is central to the character of Odysseus and to the artist as well. Accomplishment is never final; life's journey only ends with death. The Sirens here play the

role of dangerous muses calling the hero forth to new adventures. That Hope chooses this poem to begin his *Collected Poems,* which otherwise observes a definite chronological ordering, indicates the irony of the title, that the call here is to a new journey.

This identification with Ulysses (not least reinforced by the fact that Hope's marriage of long-standing was to a woman named Penelope) is sustained over the years and provides a wonderful symmetry until about Hope's seventieth year. The concluding poem of his book, *A Late Picking,* published in 1975, was "Spatlese" (*LP,* 87), which begins with an aged man tasting his wine while overlooking his vineyard. He muses to his satisfaction that his vintage has "caught the grace I aimed at as a lad" but catches himself up with further consideration: "Yet ripeness is not all."

He goes on to contrast the ambitions of youth and old age. Whereas "Young men still seek perfection of the type" the aged sense what transcends the particular: "A grace that lies beyond, one learns in time." The poem thus becomes a call to action in old age, concluding that "Old men should be adventurous" and citing Tolstoy and Ulysses. In Hope's old age, Ulysses is no longer moping at the shore but is ready for new odysseys. Another element of this poem that demands attention is the implicit rejection of the heroic for the mythic. Since Ulysses can partake of both realms, perhaps a poem in which he appears is not an inappropriate place for them to meet.

As a younger poet, Hope developed an aesthetic of power discussed in the previous chapter, people exerting their humanness to the utmost: "Young men still seek perfection of the type." But as an older, wiser, and in some ways calmer poet, Hope has come to seek transcendence, the "grace that lies beyond," which is the substance of myth. G. A. Wilkes noted that Hope "who had begun by testing the world against an heroic standard may have come to question the standard itself" (147). The gods are not to be conquered—they are to be seduced to human use through each age's reworking and recasting of timeless myths, revised to speak to the present condition.

Thus many of the myths are altered substantially. Another poem that makes use of a Homeric motif is "Circe" (*CP,* 71), although a painting by Dosso Dossi provides the immediate inspiration for the poem. In this poem it is Circe herself who is the ultimate captive, cut off through her own incantations from human society. She finds she is also "transfigured by the hideous spell" and that as she loses the capability of "human speech, / For the first time her heart is rich with words." When she

attempts to break the spell, she is unsuccessful in restoring the humanity she took away; the "lonely island and the sounding beach / Answer with barks and howls, the scream of birds." Circe becomes the artist trapped in her art, the cold experimenter whose magic art or science cuts her off from meaningful human contact.

Another god in a Hope poem who discovers his actions have unforeseen consequences is Prometheus. In "Prometheus Unbound" (*CP*, 89) the chained god is still unconquered in spirit when Hermes swoops down to strike off his chains. Prometheus refers to Zeus as the "old tyrant" and asks whether he has had a change of heart or has ceased to rule. Hermes responds by citing verbatim the speech of Zeus on Prometheus's extended though altered punishment in which Prometheus now shall wander through the " 'ashes of mankind' " and ponder " 'that theft of fire from which they died.' " Such an alteration could once have seemed arbitrary, but with the advent of the nuclear age (the poem was written in 1954) the retold myth speaks to our predicament. The gift of a god can be perverted into a tool of destruction.

Probably the most successful of Hope's transformed myths is "Faustus" (*CP*, 202), in which Hope is able to bewail contemporary life far more successfully than he does in many of his satires. The poem begins faithful to the Faust tradition, starting just after Faustus's fatal signature, and spends some verses detailing the conversation between the Doctor and the Devil. Then Faustus's remaining 24 years are telescoped, recounting how he "wondered sometimes at so little done" and does not note just how he has already been undone; being able to simply wish and have that wish fulfilled has undermined his will. He has lost the fullness of human emotions, sensed his "reason atrophy" and "Love decay / Untried by passion, desire itself grow stale." Faustus's mighty dreams have come to nothing, and he has become a "petty conjurer" who uses Mephistopheles' skills and fails to develop his own.

At last the final midnight arrives and Faustus waits in dread, but Satan does not appear. Come morning, the jubilant and unbelieving Faustus races down the stairs to the street and bumps into the devil. Faustus thinks this is the end certainly but Mephistopheles assures him that they already possess his soul; in fact they " 'took your final payment months ago.' " He then counsels Faustus that he won't miss his soul, but this was clearly too much for Faustus to bear; perhaps it is easier to deny the soul altogether than to make it a material that can be foreclosed. What had been a theological choice was now more a matter for bankers; such a world was worse than the hell Faustus thought he'd have to bear.

Returning to his tower, Faustus finds it barren, draws his knife, and finally finds Helen: "Ten thousand years of knowledge were in her eyes / As first he cut her throat and then his own." Compared to the loss or devaluation of the human soul, all the pyramids that Faustus could have erected were of no worth.

The poem also speaks in a subtle manner to Hope's personal situation, his sense that his profession was keeping him from his true work. As Kevin Hart astutely observes, "Hope turns to Faustus to help him broadly interpret his sense of existential doubleness—his dual life as poet and professor" (87). Whereas one would not necessarily think of these roles as being in conflict as much as, say, Kafka's days in the office and nights writing, still the dramatic increase in publications following Hope's retirement indicates otherwise.

The reason myth is so infinitely adaptable is that it has its roots in ordinary experience, in local roots that often seem unheroic; Yeats's "foul rag-and-bone shop of the heart" is where the mythical ladder begins. Hope acknowledges this fact in a minor poem, "The Apotelesm of W. B. Yeats," which lists such commonplaces as milkmaid and blackbird and then claims "The Muse was there." From the mundane "Sheep in the meadow, / Cows in the corn" comes the true: "Out of such moments / Beauty is born." For it is the artist who is the mythmaker. The common materials of the world are not so common after all when seen through the transforming eye of the poet.

This is perhaps most clearly evidenced in the epistolary poem "Girl with Pigs" (*AOR,* 53). The poem is presented as a series of letters between the Earl of Ossory and Sir Joshua Reynolds. Ossory possessed a painting of Venus that, he thought, might be a Titian, but was badly in need of cleaning. He asked his friend, the painter Reynolds, to clean it for him; Sir Joshua replied that he would on one condition: Ossory must accept the Gainsborough painting "Girl with Pigs" that Reynolds owns as surety. If Reynolds should damage the "Venus" while repairing it, the "Girl with Pigs" would be Ossory's to keep.

Reynolds considers the relation between the two paintings, remarking on the disparate nature of the subject matter, the contrast between the goddess and the farm girl. But Reynolds then goes on to discuss the illusory nature of assigned value, the fact that minus their subjects' clothes and titles, these would simply be portraits of ordinary, attractive women. Nature, he asserts, has an eye not sworn to the confines of human titles: "Without our titles . . . . . .We are but flesh." This is the voice of the demythologizer, a voice one would expect to be a busi-

nessperson's, not a painter's. And it was not typical of Reynolds, whose argument for the Grand Style in his *Discourses* stands in opposition to this point of view.

Ossory immediately catches him up in a postscript to the letter the Earl writes in reply and teasingly asks whether it might not be better to reverse the argument. The job of the artist is to make the girl with her pigs a Circe, not to make Venus simply a naked body. Art for Hope is as much a way of seeing as it is technical execution. Poetry is an act of seeing one thing in terms of another, the universal and the particular, the timeless and temporal in embrace. The artist is the mythmaker.

In his poem "Romancero" (*Ant,* 68), Hope outlines how myth grows from the ordinary to the extraordinary. A botched, minor incident in history over time and in the hand of poets "Becomes more glorious than most victories." The speaker remarks that "History gives way to epic" and that the heroic emerges from the commonplace. The poem examines further the transition of epic into high romance, how a small band of Basque bandits gives way to a "countless Saracen host," how Roland's sword Durandal became a "valiant Knight," and numerous additional motifs. But then the mythologizing process is reversed when scholars rediscover the actual events that transpired; literal truth is served, but at a considerable cost to the imagination. The epic and romance genres have been displaced by "sober History." Indeed, Hope, in a much earlier poem, "Observation Car" (*CP,* 22), wants to be "a poet and not that sly / Anus of mind the historian." Yet Hope does not argue against history; he argues against the tyranny of fact that denies the imagination, that there are greater truths than the literal and "Time has an end whose end is not in time."

Hope is not pleading here for an obscurantism that ignores the modern world to return a sense of meaning and mystery to existence. As I shall explore in the next chapter, Hope is very much interested in science, in our expanding knowledge of the workings of the physical world. But what he is vitally concerned about is another kind of knowledge, "Rhyme / Whose truth is vision." Here we see the direct linkage between poetry and myth: that reality cannot be reduced to mere fact.

In *Native Companions* Hope noted how central to the individual is this connection between myth and poetry. He remarked that in early childhood "we create our myth of the world and our own dance of language which expresses and celebrates the myth. By 'myth of the world' I mean that picture of the way things and people are which differs from every other person's picture, and both reflects and helps to form what we call

an individual, a unique person or personality. All art, and poetry more than other arts, is the product of this personality and the expression of its individual myth" (8). And also key for Hope is the implicit understanding that the individual myth becomes a part of the general myth.

Hope continually stresses the idea of community, of the inherent linkage of the arts and the fullness of knowledge, and emphasizes the role of the artist as a person speaking to people as opposed to the solipsistic nature of much contemporary poetry. Leonie Kramer, writing of Hope's book, *A Midsummer Eve's Dream,* noted: "His whole argument in the book depends on accepting the notion that poetry is . . . the repository of mythological stories which have deep psychological relevance to the everyday life of human beings" (28). Probably the poem in which Hope most explicitly and most thoroughly examines the role of myth is that central but flawed work "An Epistle from Holofernes" (*CP,* 58).

The poem begins with the speaker addressing his lover; he soon assumes the role of the ghost of the slain Holofernes and speaks to his lady as if she were the still-living Judith. He warns her that to pacify his spirit, though he wishes to do her no harm (despite the fact that she cut off his head), she must perform rites to supplicate the spirit of Holofernes. This leads naturally enough into a long soliloquy on the role of the mythical once the speaker returns to his own voice; for most of the rest of the poem the voice of the dead commander is dropped in favor of the lover addressing his love. "Holofernes" is central to any consideration of Hope's work; the irony is that the work demands our examination despite the fact it is an unsuccessful poem. G. A. Wilkes notes that "Although the doctrines enunciated in 'An Epistle from Holofernes' are obviously important to Hope, they are not made dramatically relevant to the situation with which the poem itself deals" (146). In other words, almost any mythological couple would be as appropriate to the poem as Holofernes and Judith, many probably more so. The bulk of the poem examines how we need myth to live; it has nothing to do with Judith and Holofernes.

The speaker recognizes that myth no longer has the immediate power it once had. Writing from this awareness, he states that in the past the mind had "certainty to conjure with" and "the saving ritual of our myth." The saving ritual took the form of a religious rite; there was a different ritual for each occasion that gave coherence to the world and form to behavior. Myth no longer speaks to us in such a direct way; it does not free us from dread and has thereby lost its ritualistic signifi-

cance. Probably the most important element of any ritual is the sense of catharsis available to those who fervently believe in the rite; ceremony, if entered into genuinely, relieves the individual of that heavy sense of guilt and isolation that is otherwise inescapable. The traditional Catholic confessional served a similar function. Conservative protestants such as the Puritans attempted to shift the burden of conscience easing onto public confession. A living ritual was not only more effective psychologically, it was also relatively easy for the penitent.

Myth retains its value in the contemporary world as "it confirms / The heart's conjectures" and stands the routine that "masks us from ourselves." And in revealing us to ourselves as microcosms, myth informs us of our place in the macrocosm, our role "in the Great Design," informing us of "the truth of what we are." Myth, in short, is that which keeps us from being merely what we seem to be. All individual facts make us particular; myth shows what we share with the cosmos.

Hope then puts the visible realm of the mythic in the night sky, placing the matrix of the mind's symbols in the outward mental play of the constellations. It is easy to see why Hope chose the night sky. The stars are largely named and grouped according to mythological sources. Beyond this, the night is a time of mystery and contemplation. The sky impresses its vastness, its otherworldliness, much more forcefully by night than during daylight hours. And it also invites another of those dualities that Hope finds irresistible and that sets him at odds with most postmodernists: if night is of the mythic, that which transcends this world, then day is of this world; while myths are "Freed from the sun of custom" they can inform what "the daylight vision of the tribe" merely sensed. But these myths must be remade for modern people who are sinking ever lower in the swamp of cynicism. The natural remaker of myths is, not surprisingly, the poet who must "gather in the visionary grain." Hope is more cautious in "Holofernes" than he was when dealing with the heroic. The hero rejects difference by attacking it—the other poses a threat. Likewise, the lovers trapped in the physical turn love into war. But the mythic is not an attempt at exclusion; what is transcendent is at least partly dependent on that which it transcends. The roots of the mythic are firmly in the earth; the tree that reaches toward the heavens sends its roots deep into the ground. In the same way, the world of daylight is not to be rejected because those who put too much faith in fables "Lose the real world, plain sight and common touch." Any approach that denies its polar mate leaves searchers incomplete, missing "Half their salvation."

Next follows an unfortunate passage in which books turn vampires, and Hope vainly tries to reintroduce Judith and Holofernes to the poem. These failures are only partly redeemed by the description of the power of myth that the persona offers. Though the "world we lost grows dim," the sky arching overhead still offers guidance. Hope then switches his basic metaphor a bit disconcertingly, stating that myth provides a contrast to our arid existence, pointing to the water that lies under the desert. The mythic sustains in a manner that is often nearly subliminal; one thinks of Frost's remark that poetry reminds us of that which it would impoverish us to forget, a comment Hope would readily second.

The poem concludes with an argument that both day and night vision must be embraced, that we must learn a "Vision that keeps the night and saves the day." The two ways of seeing must be kept in balance. Once again we see the importance of oppositions for Hope. The irony is that this poem, which is central to understanding Hope, is so highly flawed that Ruth Morse chose to exclude it when she edited Hope's *Selected Poems* published by Carcanet in 1986.

"Soledades of the Sun and Moon" (*CP*, 106) is a slightly more successful poem dealing with the mythic and attempting to overcome dualism while still depending on it as a means for couching abstract terms. It is worth noting here just how far visionary writing, writing attempting a sort of mystical union, is removed from the satirical mode. Satire exists by contrast; one assumes a rational mean from which the subject matter of the poem, the target for the satirist, has deviated. Satire is reasonable, but it is not tolerant. That which is other is more than likely derided. The mythic, however, is an attempt to embrace the other.

"Soledades" has its flaws, but they are different from those of "Holofernes." Whereas the concrete choice of a particular myth, because it was the wrong myth, doomed the latter poem, the former is too abstract; though it is filled with objects, it is grounded in none. What the reader is given instead seems at times a bewildering catalogue. There are 10 verses, all of which read like the first with its catalogue of "primal energies" and the "twelve metaphysical creatures" that rejoice as "the year walks among the signs of heaven, / Swinging her large hips." Like some passages of Blake's prophetic books, there is a great deal going on here, and little is given to the reader to help unlock the puzzles the poem poses. This is quite unusual for Hope; when he displays his faults, they are usually ones of overexplicitness.

Nevertheless, there are elements present here that make parts of the poem worth deciphering. After numerous semi-invocations, the persona

calls on Apollo, the god of poetry, to heal the separateness of existence, to "Join these divided hearts" and help "The raving sybil and the lucid seer" discover lyrics for "the one music, each revealing / Light in the other's dark." The night sky is again the realm of the mythic, and music is the dominant motif of "Soledades." Music is an important harmonic symbol of unity for Hope, as we shall examine in a later chapter. The nature of Apollo is double as well. Although he is to bring about the joining of the divided hearts, Apollo is a destroyer as well as an artificer. But it is he who gives that power peculiar to poets, the power of song.

Poetry, love, and music are intertwined with myth throughout the remainder of the poem, which is saved from its dimmest obscurities mainly by rhetoric. In such a maze of images, rhetorical devices are the organizing principle. Eventually, the speaker is able to exhort his lady to be his "Circe—or be my Queen of Sheba" and allow their love, like poetry, to drink from the unity of existence available in myth. The skeptic might wonder how this lover, who is presumably not a poet, might partake of the chalice "From which the poets alone drink wisdom," but such minor loose ends are really not a concern in a poem of such sweep.

Hope is arguably more successful when he is able to ground his concern in a particular myth that is more apt than that of Judith and Holofernes. He rewrote the myth of Apollo and Daphne twice. In the second version (*LP*, 70), after Daphne's transformation in his hands, Apollo hears a ghostly voice speak to him, informing him that despite losing Daphne he has won the power to "sing that metamorphosis!" and that in this ability "men share in the divine." The human as creator, as artist, is most godlike; conversely, god as artist is most human. Apollo obeyed the instruction he received, wrote his song, and "found his triumph in this."

This theme is explored more fully in "Orpheus" (*O*, 1), where it is also love that leads to a more profound music. When young, Orpheus was a poet who made his "Effortless music" of "Spontaneous echoes." It is only after the loss of Eurydice that he discovers the "ultimate measure of menace and dread" that allows him to learn "another music" to which the "whole world answered" and to discover the fullness of harmony. So Orpheus would not lead all humans into "that delirium," Bacchus crazes the women of Thrace to kill him. Art, in its full encounter with truth, poses danger to lesser amusements. After the Thracian women destroy him, Hope exclaims "It was too late!" But one quickly sees this refers not to the demise of Orpheus but to the immortality of his song, that "poets renew its deathless harmony." The final song of Orpheus becomes

the poet's burden and blessing, makes poetry a repository of living myth, and gives birth to one of the memorable poems of Hope's later years.

In "Soledades" Hope writes of his "lark arising or your dove descending." As the poet sings like the lark and partakes of the divine, the god in classical mythology usually descends out of love, or, perhaps more accurately, lust. Some human beauty catches the god's interest and he is not satisfied until he possesses her. "Jupiter on Juno" (*Ant,* 63) is a monologue delivered by the god after he has been upbraided by his wife following one of his many dalliances with nubile human beauties. He complains of Juno that she knows a great deal, but there is still something she does not realize. The reader is more fortunate than Juno because Jupiter's knowledge is then offered in the poem.

He finds the goddesses tedious because of their insulation from mortality; that they "never took a risk in all their lives" leaves them "Complacent virgins and self-righteous wives." Juno thus cannot comprehend the fascination that Jupiter feels for his doomed human lover, a woman who even "at her peak and prime / Senses her beauty doomed to the abyss." The human woman must take chances and she, "daring the unknown, achieves [the] sublime"; a comparison with Hope's poem on the antechinus would not be as inappropriate here as it might first appear.

Ironically, the very fact of physical mortality and decay that leads to loathing and disgust in such poems as "Rawhead and Bloody Bones" or "The Dinner" is here the foundation of the attraction felt by the immortals. What attracts Jupiter is the continual striving of humankind, its aspirations to be more than what it is. This makes possible the meeting with the other; although the god commits a rape, it is he who is seduced. Our mortality, which could plunge us into despair, also motivates us to create, to overcome the silence of *ennui,* much as Keats believed. Thus Jupiter next links the arts of love and poetry—through these doomed loves he has discovered the essence "which broods / In mortal poetry's similitudes." As art strives for the immortal, the immortal strives for art. The poet, in tempting humankind away from the temporal, tempts the gods to humankind. Jupiter reaches to mortal women from his lack, and they accept him from theirs, he toward their "tender, dark mortality" and they "groping to discern my numen."

But the transactions between human and god are not exclusively confined to male gods seducing female humans. Despite the pleas in "Soledades," most gifts of immortal song are given by goddesses. (The

most likely reason for this is that, historically, the overwhelming major-
ity of poets have been male.) In "The Wild Bees" (*Ant,* 41) Hope retells
the story of how Pindar received the gift of song from Persephone. After
meeting her in his dream, Pindar awoke to discover that his lips were
sealed by wax from the wild bees. Upon breaking the seal he composed
"the first of all his songs." Pindar, however, forgot Persephone who,
10 days before his death, reappears to him to upbraid him that she who
had made him a poet had not been the subject of any of his poems and
tells him that he shall make one for her after he dies, " 'when you come
to me.' "

After his death, the ghost of Pindar returns and sings the song he has
made for Persephone to a relative who had memorized all his songs.
Only the first three words of the poem remain today, *"Potnia, thes-
mophore, chrysanion* ("Lady, bearer of rites, golden-reined"). Hope then
addresses Persephone directly and muses on his own fate and beliefs as a
poet, that even in his old age he continues to practice the "ancient
superstitions" that "Stir intuitions" of other forms or modes of life.
Although his analytic mind remains uncertain of these possibilities, his
intuition pushes him toward affirmation through his art: "I sense their
presences in earth and air." He then speaks of his joining with Persephone, that he will bring her this poem and taste the "Black honey" that
is sustained by poetry and "share its resurrection with the corn."

The source of the poet's art calls the poet back. This vague sense of
"presences" is all that we can affirm as the reality behind myth. Yet this
sense is at least psychologically real since it is the source of all art that
claims the transcendent.

A poem similar to "The Wild Bees," though taking place amid the
brutalities of this century, is "In Memoriam: Osip Mandelstam, December 1938" (*LP,* 79). Mandelstam, near death in a labor camp, is given a
"spade / To dig a hole in Asia" but he is spiritually far removed from the
horrors of the scene of which his body is still a part. His mind no longer
distinguishes the particulars of his specific historical situation from the
timeless myths, that time near death when "time and space reel inwards
and collapse." He confuses Petersburg and Troy, remembers Cassandra
but is uncertain whether "in Troy or in Tashkent?"; time and art run
together in moments of visionary transcendence. The "reality" of his
desperate situation can impress itself upon him for but a moment;
though Mandelstam is reminded of his imprisonment by the harsh voice
of a guard, as soon as he places his foot on the shovel's edge he senses
that "Persephone's bees" emerge from the hole he is digging in the

frozen ground. He then offers her his song, that he is coming to her as
Pindar did, having " 'learned at last the art of coming home.' "

Persephone, of course, is of all the gods the one whose existence is
most dualistic. It is interesting to note that Mandelstam's hell is on
earth while Persephone's is under it in the caverns of Dis; indeed, the sit-
uations of gods and humans are usually a mirror for each other. Nevertheless, their interdependence must be stressed. From the dark world,
the underground, the unconscious, comes the gift of song to the world
of light and consciousness. The world of myth underlies the world of the
factual, plays night to its day.

In another of Hope's retold myths it is made clear that even Persephone's situation is not unambiguous; just as the speaker in
"Holofernes" warns his listener not to abjure either daylight or darkness,
in "The Return of Persephone" (*CP,* 88) the " 'Queen of the Dead and
Mistress of the Year' " discovers her leave-taking of Dis is not as easy as
she assumed it would be. As she leaves hell, she turns again to look at
her kidnapper–husband and notices that the "eyes of Dis were shut
upon their pain," that all his godlike abilities "could not mask his deep
despair." To see Dis undone in this matter brings about an epiphany for
his seasonally captive bride: "For the first time she loved him from her
heart." Persephone, living half her life in darkness, must affirm the darkness with the light. For the human, both the mythic and what we may
be inclined to see as mundane must be acknowledged; we live in a bal-
ancing of worlds.

Hope explained the title of his collection of essays *The Cave and the
Spring* in its introduction: "The Cave and the Spring are said still to exist
on the mountain sacred to the Muses. I have taken them to stand . . . . .
.principally for the sensory and the verbal imagination respectively"
(vii). It is also clear that they are symbols of the feminine and masculine
sexual organs. What seemed earlier to be warring forces are here united.
But this unity depends on the existence of polarities. David Kirby examines this paradox in Hope when he writes, in a review of *A Late Picking,*
that the "dualist's instinctive knowledge of the world's essential oneness
[is] a verity which the dualist must acknowledge because it is true, yet
reject because oneness is fine as a philosophical or religious concept yet
impossible to contemplate rationally and impractical so far as its applic-
ability to daily life is concerned."[2] But this is not altogether true. For
purposes of illustration let us consider *A* as the daylight vision, *B* as the
vision of the mythic night, and *C* as this "essential oneness" to which
Kirby referred. Kirby says that even though *C* may be true, it must be

rejected as unworkable. But, as we have seen, A and B are interdependent; if this is true, then they may be seen as a unit, C. In other words, the essential oneness of C is based on the opposition of A and B. Both the nighttime and daytime vision must be honored for the beatific vision to exist. Accordingly, before we consider C, we must now turn our attention to A, the daylight vision in Hope's work.

Chapter Six

The Scientific: Day

Myth must be grounded in fact as the language of poetry is grounded in the language of the shopkeeper. Ultimately, Hope realizes, for a modern myth to be created the artist must not ignore the quotidian world but must transform it. And nowhere does the presence of the factual so assert itself as in the sphere of science.

Science and poetry are rarely seen as intellectual partners in this century. The range of empirical knowledge has expanded to such a degree that not even a scientist can grasp many of the latest findings in other areas of science. Each field has developed its own terminology so that every pursuit seems to require a new language. The essential concerns of the scientific and the poetic often seem at odds; the former is supremely empirical, the latter anything but empirical in common practice today. The poet has turned inward, more concerned with his or her own moods than with order in the universe. And, Hope would argue, the poet has thereby lost the world.

Indeed, Hope has claimed that the "treasures of knowledge, the vast new resources for the poetic imagination which lie in the discoveries of science, remain practically untouched by creative writers" (*Cave,* 92). He is more outspoken in *The New Cratylus:* poets "have simply failed to keep up with the transformation of the whole universe which science has achieved in the last century" (168). He goes on to state that "Nobody now goes to poetry to learn anything about the world in which we live. Its function, as stated and believed and practiced from Aristotle to Dryden, 'to instruct and delight', has lost the leg called instruction. . . . We do not go to the poets to learn about the world we live in because they don't *know* anything about it that we don't know ourselves" (168).

How does a poet approach this most forbidding field? One reads textbooks, not poetry, to gain scientific knowledge. Hope argues against too literal an approach to science as a subject for poetry. He refers to "all those rather tedious eighteenth century . . . versified accounts of Botany or Medicine, or do-it-yourself handbooks in verse on how to make cider or raise sugar-cane." He allows that such endeavors constitute a "false direction"; the task of the poet is obviously not to chronicle the progress

of science as would a textbook but to "elicit its proper music, to make us feel the power and delight of what this knowledge adds to our concept of the world and of human life in it" (168–69).

This still leaves us with a clearer idea as to what poetry should not do rather than what it should do. In the last chapter, I considered the contrast between the night vision of the mythic and the day vision of what most people would be inclined to term reality. Hope both expands and refines this idea in the central metaphor of an essay entitled "Day-time and Night-time Vision" in which he states that the poet is "concerned not with analytic knowledge but with eliciting what the medieval philosophers called the *quidditas,* the *whatness* of things."[1] This begins to sound like a merging of Duns Scotus and the objectivists until Hope offers his guiding analogy of "day-time and night-time vision. We actually see with different parts of our retinas in daylight and in darkness and the night-time vision is not nearly so precise and clear." As such, the daylight vision is "infinitely superior, more exact and precise." So far this is an argument a scientist might advance. The information given is biological, its truth optically verifiable.

However, Hope immediately adds, "But it has one limitation":

> Had the human race grown up in a world continually illuminated by the sun it would have considered the earth, the sun and the moon to be the whole universe. . . . I believe that the poets, that artists in general, have another kind of vision, that the imagination is an instrument of seeing and apprehending, and that its function is constantly to be enlarging the scope of the scientists' vision. (182–83)

This vision is not composed solely of information, raw data to fuel the latest scientific formulation. It is a different kind of knowledge, but it is not to be separated from the scientific sphere in the way that poetry is cut off today. Rather, it is the complement of the scientific, just as night is the complement of day. It is an extraction of music, the music of myth, from the same materials from which the scientist extracts data. Hope claims that poetry is a necessary counterpart of science; despite this fact, "poets have largely failed to live up to their possibilities. They have renounced their function and withdrawn from the intellectual adventure we call science" (182–83). The knowledge that is the special province of the poet is rooted firmly in the world of fact; the poet's task is fulfilled simply by being true to his or her material but realizing that that material is not confined to the poet's mind alone. Hope also

believes that poets should include in their canons of themes confrontation with those issues that scientific research brings to the consciousness of modern humans. Otherwise, poets are not really being true to their materials because they are ignoring the "intellectual adventure we call science," which is probably the most important intellectual adventure of our time.

This is not a case of a poet's theory proclaiming one truth and his or her poetry pursuing another, but Hope was late in coming to this concern; he had to express it in his criticism before he made a place for the scientific in his poetry. Many poems of his middle age were concerned with the rhetoric of power, of overcoming the world rather than understanding it; it is also worth noting that all of the poems to be discussed in this chapter were written after Hope had turned 60.

Leonie Kramer makes this point in 1979 when she takes an overview of Hope's career and says that his "early poems announce his characteristic subjects and interests" and convey a "central emotional turbulence" with the "poet's strenuous attempts to examine the implications of his developing ideas and to come to grips with the realities of his own nature." She then goes on to comment: "however, Hope's poetry has on the whole tended to move away from the contest with that reality. There has been an increasing disposition . . . to seek out subjects which provide the opportunity for discoursing on abstract topics, philosophical problems, or modern scientific theories" (14).

But is this preoccupation with the scientific and philosophic really the retreat that Kramer intimates it is? Rather, I think this shift is an attempt to come to terms with a physical reality that seemed to produce poems of disgust such as I examined in the chapter on the grotesque, that these new poems may be as much the fruition of this disgust successfully overcome as the result of the cooling of passion with age. As an example, advancing years have not changed Hope's poetic delight in sexual love. Fundamentally, the victory of the mythic over the heroic modes as indicative of an acceptance of this world, is, in effect, an expansion of dualities. The polarity of mind and body has given way to a grander duality, the temporal and the timeless. The poet's right concern is with the timeless, but, as seen in the previous chapter, the timeless is rooted in time.

Scientific developments are important to poetry because they are important to humans in general. Scientists, through their study of the material universe, have changed our conception of the world and thereby altered it for us. Any transcendent view that does not deal with

the scientific does not deal with the physical world in which a metaphysical vision must be rooted. Poets have by and large shirked the challenge this age of science has presented them:

> It seemed to many in the nineteenth century that not only religion but the whole field of mythology, the pasture of poets, was being destroyed by the discoveries of science. The poets of a later age have had to find another view in which the mysterious bow of God's covenant with man remains valid for the imagination and is not touched by what the sciences of optics and meteorology tell us.[2]

Yet Hope also acknowledges that there is a certain inherent conflict between the poetic and the scientific mind and that this conflict must be recognized so that each discipline can offer the other the respect they both deserve. In a lengthy but light poem, "Poor Charley's Dream" (*LP,* 7), Hope satirizes the effort by C. P. Snow, the British novelist and scientist, who in his book *Two Cultures* attempted to reunite the sciences and the humanities. After a rather embarrassing dinner in which he was seated between a "senior wrangler" and a "rabid Leavisite," Charley Snow begins to consider the gulf into which he had fallen and decides that the "time, not he, was out of joint." There is a disunity in the contemporary life of the intellect, with "Science and Letters out of touch," a gulf that should be bridged.

Charley writes his thesis and retires to bed, when, in a dream, he is summoned to "Dame Nature's Parliament." Nature calls this separation of the two disciplines a " 'double blessing I designed / For the improvement of mankind.' " She describes how she works in dualities and developed them to the point where " 'two sexes led the dance / Of choice, variety and advance.' " From the development of these polarities come those qualities that lift the human past the merely animalistic by elevating " 'Mere sexual drive to mutual love.' " She goes on to explain that when science was confused with art both disciplines were compromised with " 'Angels performing aerobatics' " and " 'Science lost on fairy ground.' "

Snow ignores this dream, but Hope clearly does not. Not only does he create poetry from dualities, but for Hope a transcendent view is only possible from an appreciation of difference. It can sometimes be difficult to apprehend exactly the sort of truth that poetry can claim as its province. What is clear, as already stated, is that poetry's knowledge is of a different kind than that of science, though it operates from consideration of the same materials.

And here Hope reverses the usual pattern. Poets such as Keats had seen science usurping the universe from poetry. What Hope often does is not ask directly what poetry can do but ask what science cannot. If the two realms claim different forms of knowledge, then science cannot really usurp the essentials of poetry. The inadequacies of science can show the strengths of poetry. As a result, Hope's successful poems dealing with scientific matters often illustrate the limitations of science while at the same time applauding the creative search of the scientist, which is also the search of the artist. Hope's less successful works in this vein are those that try to appropriate too much of the material of science.

The most common failure of Hope's science poems is a glibness, a display of wit and arcane knowledge, arcane at least to the layperson. We have already seen this tendency in chapter 3 with poems such as "Morning Coffee." An example of this from poems dealing with science can be seen in the concluding verse of "Adam Ben Googol" (*LP*, 53) in which Adon, quarks, quasars all appear as do such lines as "Let arche be chaos, the gate is 'quantum suff.' " One senses that Hope is enjoying himself here, but the poem might better have remained a private exercise. Such poems simply do not yield rewards proportionate to the effort they demand of the reader.

Hope's rewarding efforts see science in dimensions of humanity. An example of this is "Exercise on a Sphere" (*LP*, 19). The speaker is alone in a room in which a Christmas party has just been held. The party was successful, but now the persona is suffering from postparty depression. He then notices he is not really alone, that he sees his reflection in a Christmas ornament, a silver ball. He remarks of the reflection in the ornament that the "lips twist back in a non-Euclidean grin" and the "bulbous nose is a parody of my own"; the face stares out from an alien world that "ghosts of Bolyai and Cayley, Gauss and Klein / Have distorted." This other world is a geometer's nightmare where "there is no straight line" and "there are no fixed shapes any more."

The speaker moves closer to examine the ornament and is greeted by an "insect voice more daunting than a shout." What the voice says is even more unsettling; it is strident in its dismissal of the man, first summarizing the human's thoughts that the world within the ball must seem " 'a grotesque' " or a " 'crazy fiction' " but then claims superiority for his nonlinear universe where " 'Nothing is arbitrary.' " The voice then raises the possibility that the human world is the mirror, a " 'world of terror without limit or bound.' " He claims the finite world of the

globe is safer, much to be preferred to the other, which " 'is a nightmare from which I wake only to scream.' " The world of the sphere is the safe world, secure from the tyranny of endless space, the world we accept as true that is a " 'sphere whose radius is infinity.' " The bulb goes on to challenge the man, claiming the world outside the bulb is false, a " 'grotesque projection' " of the " 'fiction of an infinite straight line,' " and then taunts the man to disprove it.

The man is urged to step in " 'over the threshold' " and to look back at the world he's left behind and see that human conventions " 'are all distortions, your art, your morals, your law.' " For the reality is, claims the ornament, that " 'yours is the small world still; / History changes your systems like a cloak." The human is thrown into a world of complete relativity; the very otherness of the world that has been thrust upon him by the bulb has caused his own world to lose meaning. If one is ignorant of other modes of existence, his or her own is not as likely to be questioned. But the human condition is not to achieve the security one thinks wisdom should bring. The Christmas ornament taunts that humanity's " 'need for certainty is a disease past cure' " and that he better accept that " 'Christmas is over, Christmas is over at last!' "

The old systems of belief have been destroyed with nothing to replace them. Science has altered the nature of the way we perceive the world but has offered no coherent vision to sustain us. Our prolonged infancy, our Christmas, is over.

"Exercise on a Sphere" is a powerful and eerie poem, reminiscent of an Escher lithograph. Even in its prevailing metaphor, as fanciful as the events may sound, the poem is not out of step with the scientific theorizing with which it is indirectly concerned. Physicists "know" that quantum theory is correct—it works. It has led to the creation of lasers and the computer. But it cannot account for gravity. Contemporary string theory can reconcile the two, but string theory can work only in a universe that has 10 dimensions. The world of the ornament sounds more plausible all the time.

However, "Exercise on a Sphere" does not contain Hope's most typical poetic statement on science. The very title suggests the poem as experiment; the sphere is both the world of the ornament and the world itself. Yet it must be admitted that Hope rarely finds much solace in the discoveries of science; what he seems to admire more, paradoxically, is the quest that uncovers these disquieting truths and, perhaps most of all, the truths that are not discovered. Hope's muse at times seems to be the muse of the gaps, much like the god of the gaps brought about by

the eighteenth century's habit of ceding to God what could not be explained by science.

Different poems seem to debate each other, as if the poet hopes to resolve the issue by establishing a dialectic. Yet it should be stressed that a poet is not a philosopher, in any systematic sense of the word, and that one poem may contradict another is no problem as long as they are good poems. For instance, in "Parabola" we have already seen the persona ready to chance fate and plunge forward. Hope also stresses that the findings of science are not all-inclusive, that while the "heart is quite predictable as a pump / But, let love change its beat, the choice is blind" and "no one knows which way the cat will jump." This rejection of behaviorism allows him the freedom to act, and action is treated as adventure. The quest of the knight becomes the quest of the scientist in the laboratory or observatory.

However, Hope does not find all investigation good; in "Kanathos" (*Ant,* 30), Hope writes of visiting the spring Kanathos where Hera restored her virginity. Addressing the poet Pausanias, who had visited the spot 18 centuries before, Hope dreams that had they been able to visit the shrine together they "would both agree / To forgo more research" as they must not "profane a mystery." Although this is a much lighter poem than "Parabola," there is a real tone of obscurantism in this work that is rare for Hope. In most cases, he is far more likely to try to reconcile myth and research than he is ready to draw back. He usually believes that further exploration does not profane but rather deepens the mystery.

"Sir William Herschel's Long Year" (*AOR,* 93) is a much more fanciful poem than "Kanathos," but it is an interesting example of the mythologizing of science. Of course, to mythologize science reverses our expectations, which adds to the delight of the poem. Hope takes an odd set of circumstances. The poem deals with Herschel's discovery of the planet Uranus, and Hope begins with the mythological root of the Uranean saga. Uranus, gelded and banished in space, has been forgotten by his wife Gaia, the Earth. To let her know of his exile and bring himself again to her mind, Uranus, once more intact (apparently things other than virginity can be restored), produces a son, William Herschel, who will discover the planet and thereby bring Uranus to Gaia's attention once more.

A year on Uranus is equal to 84 years on earth, and William Herschel lived to be 84 years old. Hope ends a madcap series of events by a defense of his myth and a debunking of the myth of science; while his

fable may be termed "trivial nonsense" by some, he says "Its truth lies in analogy, not fact," thus establishing a realm independent of scientific truth. Hope goes on to claim that it is a delusion to think "that the march of science at last will lead / To total comprehension of the whole." While Hope does not discount the importance of science—"Reason and knowledge must direct mankind"—he does assert that for scientific discovery, the "mystery deepens with each step we take." This deepening mystery seems to Hope to be more and more the realm of the poet. There is something in the nature of things that eludes definition.

Theoretical physicists, who are much more concerned with the core of matter (essences, if you will) than are most other scientists, are also more inclined to affirm the ultimate strangeness of matter; what we now conceive may be so partial as to be erroneous. Tracts of unified field theorists often seem of a kind with arcane scholastic manuscripts.

A much more fixed idea of the universe is pondered initially in "Anniversary Ode (1577–1977)" (*Ant,* 70). The poem celebrates the return of Luis de Leon, who had been imprisoned by the Inquisition for five years, to his classroom at Salamanca. The Spanish poet and teacher is rumored to have told his class, "*Dicebamus hesterna die . . .*" ("as we were saying yesterday,") upon his return. Views of the universe did not tend to reconstitute themselves with each passing generation in older eras; a universe founded on Christian precepts seemed permanent, and in the late sixteenth century a scholar such as de Leon could still imagine a world of spirits and angels, a universe in which "all is neat and near / With God in human form." This "modest universe" seems both quaint and desirable when compared with the view that we now hold.

Yet, as Hope notes, de Leon's view was already fading; in that same year, 1577, Tycho Brahe observed a comet from two different locations. Through this experiment Brahe was able to ascertain that the comet was behind the moon and that Ptolemy was in error (*Ant,* 108). The eventual rejection of the Ptolemaic system leaves us with a system more empirically verifiable but much less human. From such a universe "he has taken his leave, / Your god whose manlike image rode the storm." Our present model of the universe, if accurate, would, if it had a creator at all, have a creator utterly alien to humans. The old god was human; whether humanity was made in God's image or God in humanity's, there was a direct relationship that could be sustained. But how, when we speak of infinite space, could we relate to a god of distances so vast we cannot conceive them? The loss of a cosmological godhead also leads to a displacement of the human.

These fears are certainly not original. But here Hope argues against an obscurantism and indicates that the Spaniard would not have sought to hide from our age's scientific discoveries had he been aware of them. The true intellectual would not let him reject "Truth demonstrated plainly to be so." To be faced with such bitter truths would no more fill de Leon with despair than did his imprisonment by the Inquisition during which time his faith remained unshaken and his intellect peered "Beyond the sensory screen" to "reach the source and pierce to the unseen." Here the indication is that the source is not sensory but is "the unseen" that exists beyond the veil of science. It may therefore be in the realm of poetry.

If ultimate reality is not the physical, our interpretation of the material aspect of existence may be just our age's view of the mask that reality wears. Hope imagines a conversation between himself and de Leon in which they could discuss things discovered in the past four centuries but also contemplate what remains unknown. Within this discussion both speakers will be very much aware that the present image of the universe may be as partial as that of four centuries past. Always the search must go on, new prospects must be sought, and held beliefs, treasured or not, must be abandoned without despair; our present understandings may be no more than a child's sketch, that the "mystery merely deepens day by day." Here the same doubts that led to despair in "Exercise on a Sphere" allow for hope. Hope calls those who give their lives to intellectual pursuits "Fellows in that rare band" and their explorations a joy; at the same time he stresses the limitations of material research. The ultimate answer is elsewhere; its "source is in the heart and in the mind." Hope clearly disagrees with C. S. Lewis who held, particularly in *The Abolition of Mankind,* that with each new scientific discovery humanity is diminished. Instead, Hope again makes use of a dualistic approach: the more we discover of the physical world the more its mystery deepens.

We finally become aware that the material universe will yield no ultimate answers, not because the answers don't exist, but because we are looking at the mask rather than the reality. Scientific research is in this sense only a threat to those who fear that all meaning can be reduced to the physical. Perhaps our view of the universe may seem someday as fanciful as de Leon's, despite the fact that the contemporary view appears better grounded in observable data. Perhaps. In "The Alpha-Omega Song" (*Ant,* 53), Hope takes a guess at which of our disparate views of the universe may be most correct regarding the essence of existence and

thinks "harmony the likelier theme," a harmony that "brings us back the music of the spheres."

It is this unknowability of the universe that fosters myth, myth that is not only a celebration of the unknown but a tribute to the artist and scientist who attempt, and fail, to fathom it. Probably in no one of Hope's poems are the dual adventures of science and art seen as more of a tandem than in the poem "On an Engraving by Casserius" (*NP*, 12). Hope is nowhere more successful at drawing the mythic from the actual than in this particular poem.

The poem begins with the seekers, those who give their lives to asking questions, in what seems like a global wasteland. These scientists and artists are termed "clots of thinking molecules," hardly a picture one would usually draw in praising creation—but Hope is here insisting that the material world be observed accurately with its "night of nescience and death." The reader would expect more imagery of the wasteland to follow, but immediately the speaker shares his admiration of those who attempt to overcome their limited sphere, an attempt that "of all human images takes my breath."

The speaker then alerts the reader that the occasion for the poem is the persona's perusal of a book of scientific prints, a book of anatomy. Calling the book's makers "great cosmographers, / Surgeon adventurers," the poet sums up their goal as reaching "towards the central mystery" of our own existences. The book is from the university library at Padua, then as now a leading center for the study of medicine; the makers of the particular illustration that so attracts the speaker are Casserio and Spiegel. The poem is as meticulous in its rendering of fact as is the science with which it is concerned.

Our particular time is contrasted with the time of Casserio and Spiegel, ours being an "age in which all sense of the unique" is lost in "diagrams, statistics, tables, maps." But the speaker indicates immediately that our modern sense of abstraction had not yet corrupted their concerns, that the vision of the scientist and the artist have not yet parted. The particular is not yet lost in the general; it is clearly intimated that the major reason for this is that an "artist's vision animates the whole." The general laws are but a shadow that still allows for the unique, the individual, that which cannot be placed in charts and scientific tables.

We are then made aware that the central subject matter of the engraving is a corpse of a pregnant woman. Hope ponders her life and

notes her transformation beyond the temporal frame through the joint effort of art and science.

It is at this point that the mythologizer's eye begins to play, but only after an unblinking look at cold, objective fact. This nameless girl, this "corpse none cared, or dared perhaps to claim" with her unborn child might easily have been forgotten had she not been dissected and drawn by Guilio Casserio. Now, however, "She stands among the monuments of time." The actual dissection is described sensually, her body opening "like a flower."

The womb, cord, placenta, and embryo take on mythic qualities; they are seen as instruments left behind by Orpheus. The poet describes the corpse's pose as a "sibylline stance" and then attempts an even more daring metaphor; he first compares the woman to Eve in that she "holds the fruit / Plucked, though not tasted, of the Fatal Tree." She then seems like the second Eve, Mary, in her "Offering of her child in death to be / Love's victim and her flesh its mystic rose."

Here we have affirmation, a heavenly vision in the midst of human tragedy. The image is almost too much. Hope senses this and grounds it immediately in a way that will still elicit the same music; stressing that there was no Annunciation for this unfortunate woman, he states that she too was chosen and that under "Scalpel and forceps" her body parts "utter their magnificat." Such verse demands an act of assent from the reader, much as that of Hopkins often does. If this is merely a corpse being cut apart, the poem has degenerated into the worst kind of "poet-icism." But poets leave themselves open to such a charge any time they attempt to elevate the actual beyond the material, any time they assist in the creation of myth. The man who returns to Plato's cave is thought mad, but perhaps, to borrow Seamus Heaney's phrase, he sings "close to the music of what happens."

After the beatification of the corpse, Hope considers how four centuries of science since Casserius have still not found that for which the Paduan was seeking, that though the "patient, probing knife / Cut towards its answer" for 400 years "yet we stand in doubt." All our theories in the end prove insufficient when faced with the central reality; the great abstractions the universals "[p]ass: there remain the mother and the child." There at the center of the question are the mother and her child, the corpse and fetus become a "Loadstone, loadstar."

The scientific exploration, the autopsy, revealed new physical truths but left the mystery unanswered; it did not destroy or compromise the mystery—the explanation deepened the mystery all the more for being

unable to solve it. Science fails to reveal the "mask beyond the mask beyond the mask." One is left with silent awe before the incomprehensibility of the numinous. Hope ends the poem with an imagined speech that might be given by the mother and child stating that our "intellectual quest" may still be "but the stirrings of a foetal sleep" and heralds a new birth, a new nature when the "deep / Dawns with that unimaginable day." Certainly Hope believes the first seers of that "unimaginable day," the new shepherds minding their flocks, will be the poets whose concerns are those of the heart *and* mind.

Ours has been a scientific age and has both profited from the advantages science has given us and trembled at the threat science poses for us, both physically and spiritually. Both the scientist and the poet have a similar task, complementary rather than contradictory. The scientist adds to knowledge. The poet adds to something else:

> Poets, at any rate in this age, which is all we can be asked to answer for, are not called on to be polymaths, just to be poets, to keep and tend the delicate, inexorably extending edge of human awareness. As knowledge increases in range and complexity, making more and more demands on human abilities, consciousness must, in turn, continually extend its scope and range, and this is the physical task of poetry and the other arts, the task of 'adding to being.' (*NC,* 172)

Chapter Seven

Transcendence: Adding to Being

About halfway through "A Letter from Rome" (*CP*, 129), a long, conversational poem written in both the form and style of Byron's *Don Juan*, A. D. Hope writes of one event during his visit to Italy with a seriousness not found in the rest of the poem. That moment of special importance was when Hope retraced Byron's steps to Nemi, site of the rituals revolving around the Golden Bough. His visit united him in intent with Byron: "I like to think / What drew him then is what has drawn me now / To stand in time upon that timeless brink," and compelled him to pour a libation on the face of the water before wading out into the lake. The poet admits he was "possessed, and what possessed me there / Was Europe's oldest ritual of prayer." Although Hope's persona in the poem shrugs off the experience ("Well, let it pass: I have no views about it"), he does allow that he "sensed some final frontier passed" before returning to the brisker manner of the poem.

This is a very telling incident in Hope's work, and it is most appropriate that he stands at the threshold of the numinous by retracing the steps of an artist back to a source of Western myth. Throughout Hope's career, a remarkably consistent commitment to art, and especially the art of poetry, as a handmaiden of myth has been apparent in his work. This threshold of the numinous, the transcendent, cries for expression in the artist who has experienced it, but is of all things perhaps the most difficult to express. The transcendent is usually harder to embody in literature than is its opposite. For all the brilliance of Dante's art, his *Paradiso* is not as memorable as is his *Inferno*; we can conceive of eternal damnation much more easily than we can unending bliss. We know joy as a passing phenomenon but can well imagine pain lasting a lifetime or more. Whenever a writer seeks to impart a transcendent vision, there is always a great danger of flatness on the one hand or overstatement on the other. How can language do justice to that which transcends it? Another difficulty is that while damnation lends itself to specifics, bliss seems always abstract; again it is a matter of our being able to visualize any number of things we would not want to do, or have done to us, for eternity but having a difficult time thinking of any one thing that would

remain a joy forever. Our impressions of the truly transcendent, then, must be impressionistic, a fleeting glance at a lasting bliss we cannot conceive in detail.

It is a series of quick impressions of moments of epiphany that Hope uses in "Zion's Children" (*LP,* 26), a sonnet that begins working toward the transcendent through another duality. This time the duality is between the pleasant and solid world of mundane reality and the vague intimations of the eternal. The octave describes the pleasurable comforts of this world; the people have all their creature comforts well met. Theirs seems almost an Edenic state where "Love is for life," and they are blessed with "guaranteed health," a world of "solid joys."

But the sestet strikes quite a different note. By being so comfortable in this world, Zion's children are unreceptive to intimations from beyond. The speaker questions whether they can "understand / Moments that fall like music from a cloud" and enumerates some of the simple pleasures that, seen aright, may lead to moments of insight. These little moments, these "exquisite, transient *ephemerides,*" are not what constitute the transcendent itself but are indicators, intimations, that another world exists. It is appropriate that these hints in "Zion's Children" include references to both love and music. These two pursuits become important messengers for Hope from the beyond. Music is sound spared the burden of denotation that words must bear and ties the word to the mundane world.

The transcendent is beyond time, but we are creatures of time and therefore can only sense timelessness through intimations. Though it is customary to treat time as a continuum, time only exists in the present: the first step beyond the temporal is to sense the overpowering presence of the moment. In the poem "With Thee Conversing . . ." (*NP,* 32), Hope traces the flow of that rare phenomenon, a conversation that results in the sharing of two minds to the point at which the essential being of each conversant is touched by the other. Time seems to fade away during such talk, and the conversation itself is compared to an "enchanted stream" and "Time [is] but its pulse of dark and light." Conversation of this intensity is carried beyond words.

When the persona is alone and reflects on this rare communication he shares with another person, he finds himself nonplused as to its source or to its fate at the hands of time and has to allow "I cannot guess." But this sort of conjecture is after-the-fact theorizing; during the actual conversation nothing else exists except the present: "here my everlasting Now." As conversation, of course, the moment will fade, but

its intimations of the transcendent remain in memory—and memory is that which keeps the past present, at least temporarily preserving it from time.

A similar note is struck in "The Nomads" (*Ant,* 5). The speaker in this poem, a settled man, is debating with a nomad their opposed ways of living. As his final point, the speaker mentions death, to which the nomad responds the settled man lives " 'so rooted in time' " he has never " 'experienced an absolute moment,' " and pronounces that death is neither a beginning nor an ending but " 'each instant [must be] lived for itself.' " These "absolute moments" are all we can know of eternity. They are not servants at our beck and call but are elicited from art and love, and it is to these concerns that one must normally turn to find the transcendent in Hope.

"An Epistle: Edward Sackville to Venetia Digby" (*CP,* 157) is a lengthy poem with Sackville as the narrator. The poem is a letter that Sackville has no intention of sending, intending it rather "To cheer my more than arctic night." The particular events behind the poem are historical. Venetia Digby was promised to another, her "child-lover," but before they could marry he was reported killed overseas. She and Sackville had a passionate, though secret, affair. However, the man presumed dead returns to England very much alive and, in keeping with her word, Venetia marries him. Sackville is now reduced to an annual visit where he must seem simply a friend to the happy couple.

The poem, the "unmailed letter," is his attempt to reconcile himself to loss. At one point, Sackville wonders why he chooses to dwell so on this hopeless state of affairs. But he then decides there are larger forces at work in his canceled relationship with Digby, that the torments he suffers "are the sacrifice of love." He thinks his position on the sidelines gives him greater insight than he had as a lover; the "soul sitting apart sees what I do, / Who win powers more than Orpheus knew." This is a rather large claim to make, but Sackville speaks about a border passed in his new state as disenfranchised lover, a "gate beyond the gate," passing through which will transcend any loss. But to speak further requires going beyond the usual realm of words: "this new happiness" requires the use of fables.

Sackville then discusses how the great works of antiquity—Homer is central to his point—are now preserved in books, but he ponders how they were kept before books, while the stories were still "in the Prime," and concludes these stories of heroes were kept by most unheroic people. This legacy from the oral tradition used common men and women

as its protector; great treasures were preserved by those not entirely aware of the service they were performing. They were the vehicles for this force that Sackville next identifies with music and love: the "music of the spheres, which no man's wit / Conceives" he identifies with love through which "We serve the greater nature's need."

It should not be surprising that Hope, who talks about all art as poetry in much of his work, should, when approaching the transcendent, speak of music. Besides being compatible with the Medieval and Renaissance ideal of the music of the spheres, music is both the most direct and indirect of the arts. Music speaks most directly to people; it is usually the first art form dictators attempt to control. Yet it acts subliminally. Words and notes are both codes, but words are primarily denotative. All words have connotative qualities, some words more than others, but absolute music is nothing but connotation, though it may conform to a tight tonal structure. A poem, despite Macleish, must mean something; it exists by meaning. Music is its own meaning and thus seems most free from the particulars of this world. Music is pure sound, harmony unadulterated by the trivial circumstance.

Hope has Sackville next introduce the image, again, of a raging stream in which, in all its "ruin and rush," we see "endure / A form miraculously pure"; in the same way, humanity bears the eternal while attempting to stay afloat in this rushing, transient world. Thus the artist is responsible for the icons of the eternal. But this does not mean these images are solely at the service of the individual creator; they are "more than we" and will outlast us. They therefore are most central to our individual importance through which we grow beyond our individual selves. And then Sackville ties this back to his present situation: "thus it has been with my love."

This love, though its physical fulfillment has passed, has still lifted the lover out of the temporal, beyond the "single reach of man." This elevation is similar to that which the heroic mode sought to attain, but here it comes as a gift. This love, though now unrequited, is still a gift that cannot be taken away. It was originally rooted in the physical, but now it far exceeds the limitations of the material. Even though as lovers they once "thought they touched the pitch of grace" they now know that there was something that still remained untouched, beyond their experience. Hope then must revert to fable again to outline Nature's purpose, Nature that rewards each part of creation with "powers which transcend / Its first and fruitful purpose." One recalls here Nature reminding C. P. Snow in the previous chapter how she added love to

desire. When Nature "made / The Tongue for taste" Sackville wonders how the tongue's additional use could have been envisioned, the "improbable tale, the long / Strange fable of the Speaking Tongue?"

Again a duality is posed: the tongue, originally an instrument for animal taste, becomes the creator of poetry, the form of speech closest to music. The duality of physical nature is a continual becoming: the hand developed for plucking fruit learns the craft of the violin bow. The mundane facts of our existence are transformed; love, originally a force for "increase of kind," is transfigured into the "language of the mystery." Realizing this, the heart "resolves its chaos" and can realize the dance of the world "and through / That dance she moves, and dances too." The world, seemingly random and unjust, becomes fair and ordered; even the lost love is a gift.

But the "Epistle" poses problems as a poem similar to the earlier epistle from Holofernes, although Sackville is a more achieved poem. The context fits the meaning more than the biblical poem, but it is still difficult to believe Sackville—his pain is far more persuasive than his ecstatic vision, at least to this reader. Again, the story line seems present more as an opportunity for the poet to offer a critical position than as a dramatic situation. The poem's pontification of ideas drains the individual color from the people involved.

Hope explores similar ground in "A Mu'allaqat of Murray's Corner," in which the speaker remarks that "there are moments of time that cannot be lost."[1] Such moments are those "where the heart says: Yes!" in joyous affirmation of the world. Beyond the transitoriness of existence is the permanent source, the eternal from which the temporal drinks, where "We thought to share / The last of the wine, but the wine will always be there," the realm of the transcendental where "Nothing is lost, though brightness should fall from the air." Such lines are rhetorically brilliant, though a bit vague, but are probably as close as one can come to this sense of that numinous something that less scientific ages could call God. An empirical age does tend to cripple the metaphysical possibilities of language. The numinous can be defined specifically only in terms of what it is not; like the openings in a Henry Moore sculpture, it is an absence from which presence drinks its shape. Yet this absence is overwhelmingly there and a necessary part of the design.

It is the role of the artist to remind us of its existence. Though the arts are compromised by the temporal, they still can act as mediator between the temporal and the timeless. Hope wrote in an essay, "The Activists," that the duty of the artist was not to the state or the social

cause but was a more general obligation to humankind: "The arts establish another plane of being, a new natural order in the world. This is the task of the arts, then, to grow, to evolve new forms, to spread over the barren landscape of merely social man the mantle of their rich and various vegetation, to transform that world by filling it with a higher order of creation" (*Cave*, 36). The apposite choice of "merely social man" well underscores Hope's concern with the spirit, that territory left to the arts in a nonreligious age, at least to most of the intellectual community.

Yet art and love are not to be separated; they both are endeavors in which one senses intimations of immortality. It is not only because they play similar roles that they are so often linked together for Hope but also that one depends on the other for its existence. R. F. Brissenden remarks that Hope "regards love and art as being complementary vocations, neither in its fullness being possible without the other, although love is unquestionably the greater: life he has no doubt is always more valuable than art; and significant artistic creation can be produced only by those who are prepared to involve themselves fully and passionately in life."[2] Hope, if cornered, would probably agree with Brissenden that life is more important than art, but he most likely would be uncomfortable that the two could be separated enough to be ranked in importance.

Geoffrey Hartmann points out that love motivates Hope's poetry: "Hope's subject is love: a Venus seen in twofold vision, at once uranian and earthly. This is the love that stirs the vitals of man to rejoice in the stars."[3] This is very true but would be nearly as true if one substituted "poetry" for "love" and "Orpheus" for "Venus" in the preceding quotation. Much of Hope's early poetry displayed near nausea when confronted with the physical nature of existence. Some of it was very powerful poetry, but a transcendent vision only became possible when Hope's love of poetry and poetry of love began to work together; as Leonie Kramer notes, "Most of the poems about love from 1940 onwards refer to the transcendence of ordinary experience in love" (31). Art and love together, the two forces most powerful in Hope's life, reveal brief glimpses of the eternal. And Hope finds this "unbelievable, necessary part / Of life that is not part of living" most clearly stated in music.

The speaker in "The Young Girl at the Ball" (*CP*, 95) finds himself divinely distracted by a woman "with her full breasts and thighs" and imagines how he could have held her were he still a young man. But, being older, he has to live with his dreams and indulges himself accord-

ingly. He has visions—really daydreams—about possessing her, but it is
not long before he reminds himself that "She turns and smiles into other
eyes than mine."

Still, he can't take his eyes away from this beauty and wonders
whether he is simply torturing himself. And at last he sees the transforming call that love, like a beneficient Siren, still wills his way, that "in
every gesture I read" a calling from "the sensual miracle." A bystander
now like Sackville, he sees the essence of love as he could not when a
young lover, the sense of "a promise kept, of mysteries revealed." What
might at worst be lechery, at best a fond daydream, becomes a transcendental experience. It is appropriate that this revelation takes place while
watching the woman dance; the dance becomes an expanded dance similar to that at the end of the Sackville epistle. It hints of the cosmic
dance to the music of the spheres.

Once, at a party, Hope told the poet Gwen Harwood about a recurring dream he had. He saw himself conducting an orchestra, but he had
no music before him. Rather, he would improvise as he conducted, and
the orchestra was able to follow along perfectly; Harwood preserved this
conversation in a poem, "To A. D. Hope" (BA, 108), in which she
recounted how "themes / sprang instantly from your composing mind /
into the belly of each instrument." Hope in turn composed a poem, "To
Gwen Harwood." The poem as a response to another poem is an act of
community in itself and celebrates the commonwealth of art. Hope
remarks that whenever he hears an orchestral masterpiece, he always
sees "two dead hands still beneath the grass / With all these living hands
in their control." Such a vision reinforces not only the community of the
artist within the commonwealth of humankind but lifts the temporal
out of time and leads the flawed and partial to its place in the greater
scheme of the thinking universe.

Humanity may be fallen, but art and love redeem. Though the origin
of meaning remains a mystery, artists who honor the source find themselves and the world transformed; they are given new power and a
returned grace, a sense that "Eden is all around us." Although the poem
is written poet to poet to affirm the transcendence of the art of poetry, it
does so through musical analogy. Music is universal; it has never suffered
its Tower of Babel.

The most ambitious use of music in any of Hope's poems can be
found in "Vivaldi, Bird and Angel" (NP, 59). It is a good poem, though
not entirely satisfactory; it attempts a great deal and doesn't miss by
much. The dramatic tension is not sustained enough for a poem of this

length; it also has four speakers, two of them, the bird and the angel, hard to accept as naturally in this context as Hope would probably like.

The scene is Venice in the late 1770s; Vivaldi is conducting a rehearsal of his flute concerto, *Il Cardellino,* "The Goldfinch." The poet introduces and closes the piece. In between the reader is treated to monologues by a goldfinch, Vivaldi, and an angel who all comment on the music being played. Such a blank description certainly reveals the structural weakness of the poem, its remoteness from experience. That it is nearly successful is a tribute to Hope's modulation of voices.

The poet first indicates the religious and ritualistic nature of the music, referring to it as "miracle" or "transubstantiation" and continues with communion metaphors; the "physical sound" of music is "but the body, the outward mould, the dress." The young flutist, an attractive girl of 19, is mute but central to the poem beyond her importance of being an exceptional musician for "she / Is both their answer and the mystery." Here is revealed a central flaw in the poem; though Vivaldi later refers to her as having the "stamp of one / Got in the noble bed of Solomon / To Sheba's royal breed" and thinks her a "beauty so like music," these inferences are never picked up or developed. She is clearly meant to seem both muse and translator, or cocreator, but this remains unsubstantiated by the rest of the poem. In terms of the entire work, the "answer and the mystery" must be found in the music itself.

The poem is redeemed by many excellent passages of meditations on music, including one that ends the poet's introduction. Hope stresses both the transcendent nature of music and the sense of community possible to its celebrants, a sense of another music within the aural music. This is the mystery at the core of art and love, the transcendent hinted at by music for all to hear at any time: "I heard it as a child, I hear it now." The artist is, in many ways, merely the midwife to the truly great work of art. The empirical mind questions: "Gift? or delusion?" Acknowledging that "I cannot tell," he still stresses that, whatever this is, it joins him with the greater community of the timelessness of art, that what he hears "humbly," he knows that the "masters heard it too." This is a long way from the arrogance of the Argument of Arms ("That breed is in my bones") and reads as a sense of something shared that comes close to religion. Both art and religion reveal part of the mystery, and both have their community of believers.

Yet art and religion often speak different languages just as one mode of being is ultimately mysterious to another. The girl, composer, bird, and angel, as well as the poet who created them all, are enigmas to each

other. The bird finds the human music generally beneath that of birds as it watches the humans, "Dull grovelers at the bottom of the air." Yet as the concerto comes together, the bird is amazed to find a pleasing though mysterious music emanating from these awkward human beings and ponders whether such strange beings as humans can actually experience rapture. The bird flies off, not a moment too soon, with a trail of ellipses. Its speech is the weakest part of the poem.

Vivaldi next speaks, asking the girl for such a transcendent performance that his request sounds like Hope's dream; her body must become one with her instrument and she must become so attuned to the composer's inner thought that the music "plays itself" to where "another voice" is heard that is more than merely a sum of the ingredients of the compositional and performance process. One almost senses in this passage the language of the heroic, in particular the poem "Invocation." Vivaldi is asking in something of the manner of an invocation; the most immediate difference between the composer and the poet is that, whereas the poet need only invoke the muse for inspiration in the creation of the poem, the composer not only needs an invocation for the composition of the concerto but another to hear it successfully realized in air. The composer is more dependent on, and open to, forces beyond the self.

But if, as Hope wrote in "To Gwen Harwood," poets play that mysterious music, then this creator actually supplicates the poet, or artist generally, to give voice to this cosmic theme. As Hope wrote in another poem in the same volume, "All things solicit the poet for his art / To change dumb being into sentient wine" ("Sonnets to Baudelaire", 30). Thus the girl becomes even more central to the poem, while remaining mysterious. This could be a conscious obfuscation on Hope's part; the girl cannot speak or all would be revealed—she is mute and we cannot share her thoughts. However, when one shares thoughts with birds and angels, the girl, though silent, loses some of her mystery.

Vivaldi's monologue closes with a passage in which he describes the speech of Eden as music where "Untutored Adam raised his voice and sang" until the Fall and then Babel "brought us this / Rabble of sound." Thus the composer does not end his monologue on an affirmative note. That is for the art itself to attain, possessing a perfection not possible for the flawed human being who is the artist.

The angel's turn is next. Though Hope based its qualities on writings of Aquinas, it is not a realized character by any means. The angel finds the concerto crude but "is music still" and therefore can partake in the

music of the spheres, however humble. Human music shares in that heavenly music though it is not as rarefied. After asserting that Pythagoras was right in thinking that "All being is music," the angel then enters on a lengthy argument in verse that a being in time is a "body of sound"; music to the angels goes beyond even art and communication—it is more a way of being, a sense of unity with God. In this angelic chorus the individual becomes subsumed in God. Their "symphony / Is a great animate being" in which "all [their] energies rejoice as one."

Though the angel is a higher being than humans, humanity is ultimately unknowable to the angel. The music of angels is not art because it is their nature to "Contribute unbidden" to "the dance of being." This also hearkens back to Hope's dream of the symphony that plays itself; in "Vivaldi, Bird and Angel" the conductor can be assumed to be God, His being logically inferred from the existence of the angels.

That humanity is a mystery to the angel explains the fascination that mortals' more plodding and unnatural music holds for celestial beings. The angel knows, however, what is mysterious about humanity: "His solitude." Since the nature of angels is such that the music in which they all partake is their essential being, their lives are ones of harmony; human solitude and isolation has fallen into disharmony. Yet human music, flawed though it may be, is an attempt for their imperfect natures to overcome their isolation and share in the music of the spheres, in a "mutual ecstasy of consenting love." The community of creation joins the artists together across time and links them to Creation. Art is the effort to overcome human isolation, from other humans and from the universe.

The idea of the angel comes much closer to working in the poem than the bird but still falls short. We are perhaps asked to take too long a look at something we cannot see. The quick moments of illumination, the glimpses that bring a sense of revelation, are more workable in verse because they are grounded in the recognizable, as in "Zion's Children"; we do not see the transcendent as much as we see how our observation of the familiar material world is transformed by our added awareness. The Heavenly City is more readily accepted if we see its towers gleaming from afar; if we're given a street map, its grandeur fades to that of a plotted abstraction. Large portions of the angel's speech are saved by Hope's masterful rhetoric, but it would profit were it half as long.

"Vivaldi, Bird and Angel" closes with a coda from the poet. He rather consciously reconstructs the poem up to that point in musical terms,

but, when his musical analogy reaches its peak, he is forced to ask "who, / What then is the composer?" A note of acceptance is sounded; although the questioning human mind cannot understand this infinite music, it must admit that the music is there, so forcefully has it impressed itself upon the consciousness. The work of genius seems beyond the human, as if the artist were merely the vehicle for the timeless. But still the human mind must question, must seek as well as accept, and finds itself turned back to the source of earthly music and the human link to the cosmos, love: indeed, the poem ends invoking a scene of lovers who were each other's music in the act of love.

With an ending similar to that used in his tribute to Yeats, Hope asserts that love, the source of art and gateway to the divine, reveals the wordless mystery of life. Despite certain lapses I have mentioned, "Vivaldi, Bird and Angel" is an impressive poem; few poems written in this century have been as ambitious in scope and theme. Perhaps some of my reservations about the piece are a result of the modern ear being more attuned to poetry based on conversational English than to the music of the spheres. Yet the poem remains too abstract at too great a length; the uninspired title hints at the lack of solid imagery so necessary for a large subject.

If a poet is able in some way to preserve this feeling of divine harmony within the cacophony of daily existence, then poetry becomes an act of joy; as with Orpheus when "the heart's burden reached his lips," then the song will be sustained as "poets renew its deathless harmony" (O, 1). As Hope notes, poetry originally played a magical role in mystical religions, and, though the basic function of poetry has changed, its role as intercessor has not: "with the passage of time . . . this earlier magical aspect of poetry has passed over quite naturally into another form which still serves to feed that hunger of the heart to participate in and support the order of the world. The gnomic element in the European tradition has become the view of poetry as an act of celebration rather than an act of magical underpinning" (Cave, 15).

Such an assertion might strike the reader as a bit strange after much of the poetry discussed to this point. Yet a great deal of Hope's work is celebratory. Certainly it might be difficult to make such a case for those early poems that betray an intense disgust with the physical, but there is something of beauty even in them, in poem as a well-crafted object. For craft is in itself an act of praise, an affirmation against chaos. Hope makes clear, in another passage from his essay "Poetry and Platitude," that celebratory verse is not to be confused with mere applause:

> When I speak of celebration, I do not mean that poetry is concerned to
> be nothing but paen and praise of the natural order. It is much more
> than this. It involves not only that admiration and delight in what one
> perceives, which is the essence of praise, but also an intellectual assent to
> the causes that make the natural world an order and a system, and an
> imaginative grasp of the necessity of its processes. It is for the poet to feel
> himself to be not merely the mirror of nature or its commentator but the
> voice of creation, speaking for it and as part of it. (*Cave*, 16)

Such celebration could well include satire, since satire affirms the norm
by showing the abnormal its own face, holding that which deviates from
the natural order up to ridicule. Even in as damning a poem as "A Commination" (*CP*, 148), discussed in chapter 2, there is a certain delight in
excessive rhetoric in which the sentiments expressed are not exactly gen-
erous but have a certain joy about them; though they may have been
written in anger, one still imagines the poet having a good time conceiv-
ing his enemies' damnation. The curse has long been a delight in Irish
poetry, and even in one of the most celebratory poems in all of literature,
Dante's *Divine Comedy*, the poet rewarded friends and punished enemies
through their positioning in his grand scheme.

Still, one can sense quite a shift in attitude, at least in graciousness, in
considering "A Bidding Grace" (*CP*, 127) on the heels of "A Commination." Actually, they were written within a year of each other, so they
should perhaps be seen as complementary rather than contradictory. "A
Bidding Grace" occurs at the Last Judgment, but the poem speaks from
the point of view of the grateful supplicant who gives thanks "For what
we are about to hear, Lord, Lord," whether it be the "dreadful judgement" or the "unguessed reprieve." Whatever existence is, is affirmed:
"Lord, make us thankful to be what we must."

"A Bidding Grace" is essentially a static poem, depending on rhetoric
rather than a developing plot, image, or idea to carry it along. It is successful because of the grace of both language and concern, the large
spiritedness of mind. A few verses later, the speaker asks that he be
granted the openness of the true supplicant to whatever is judged his
lot, that he not further compromise himself through ungracious pleading—to plead is to fight against the natural order of judgment. Rather
than falling to "that abjectness which begs or sues" the speaker simply
requests: "Leave us one noble impulse: to be still." The form of the piece
is that of a selfless prayer, the structure of one verse mirroring that of the
next, and the last two lines of the poem are also parallel: the poet calls

for the saved to mourn the damned and the damned to "stand and
praise." The work is a wonderful celebration of what is and an acceptance for the role of humanity as it is. Judith Wright noted that
"Humanity . . . however its immediate manifestations may disgust and
dismay him, has for Hope been redeemed and justified by its part in the
creation and sustention of eternity" (197). Hope takes his cue from the
Italian Renaissance that humanity is most godlike through the ability to
create.

Perhaps the most obvious and sustained act of celebration in Hope's
verse can be found in "Ode on the Death of Pius the Twelfth" (*CP*, 209),
which to my mind is one of the great funereal odes of the language. Pius
XII was not everyone's favorite pope; however, the poem's ultimate
merits in this case do not rest on judgment of the worthiness of its subject. The poem begins with a statement of affirmation, that to each time
and place there is purpose and grace. At the time of the occasion the
poem commemorates, Hope was a visiting lecturer at the University of
Massachusetts and was that day walking around the campus admiring
the fall trees "in all / Their panoply of fire." As an Australian this was
Hope's first chance to see the glories of the New England fall, something he had wanted to see all his life. Hope points out the ironies that
neither spring nor summer brought such color as death now does. The
poet, as should be clear from the previous chapter, is keenly aware of the
sciences and knows that nature usually does what it does for a reason
other than aesthetics, yet these leaves seem to further no scheme of
nature by undergoing this annual process other than to delight the eye.

As he muses that "from the first spring shoots through all the year
. . . / The feast of crimson was already there," he hears one person telling
another that the pope has died. Immediately, the entire scene is transformed to a vision of the tongues of fire at Pentecost. The poet then
thinks of Pius XII, describing him as a "vast oak" of faith who stood
"Against the secular tempest" and celebrates Pius's work for peace.
These concerns, Hope claims, consumed all his time and efforts until
late in life, when "in his last years the change began." This change was
the birth of an enhanced mystical life for Pius, inner experiences that
"mark the man / Chosen and set apart." This sustains Pius through a
slow and painful death. Hope then proceeds to tie the two scenes
together, the "glorious woods and that triumphant death."

The poem next shifts to a point seven years removed from the event
when the poet ponders whether there is in the chosen a "splendour" that
is not readily visible until a state of grace is achieved when the chosen

"enter on the treasure of old age," which Hope also terms as an "autumn of the mind." The physical decay that so haunted the younger poet now can prepare the way for an existence of epiphanies, when the transient is so weakened that it allows the transcendent to manifest itself within and shine through to the outer world, now itself so transformed that the "burning soul" is beheld in "its ecstasy of fire." Despite the fact that old age often seems the weakest of stages, there is something truer, something beyond our narrow vision, a "Spirit [that] walks among us, past our ken" revealed to us in an "immense / Epiphany of light." This is a far cry from "Rawhead and Bloody Bones / Cuts himself another slice." The aging poet has grown to celebrations the young one could rarely find.

Conclusion

A. D. Hope could only have written his verse in the twentieth century; his concerns, whether they be the loss of faith, the shallowness of this commercial age, the disappearance of absolutes, or the advances of science, are addressed from a uniquely modern point of view. It is true that these were also concerns of the nineteenth century, but there is a difference in degree. The Victorian would sense certain forces as a threat but still could fall back on a structure of faith and stability as offered by the church and state. By the twentieth century, any supporting structure had been decimated, not only by "progress" but also by modern warfare. A modern artist who seeks a faith must create one for himself or herself, must construct new edifices from the ruins. This is true even for those resembling Eliot who found consolation in a traditional belief. The Anglican Church and his Royalist politics were conscious choices, not something Eliot had inherited and unconsciously accepted as part of his being.

Many artists find in their art a base of faith necessary for existence. For all his dabbling with the occult, Yeats thought himself primarily a poet. Hope, too, most often expresses his faith in his poetry; the moments of transcendence that speak of a higher reality are found for him in the analogous activities of love and art. Vivian Smith rightly claimed of Hope that "Creative achievement, effort of will, is seen as one of the ways out of the dilemma of human isolation in a world without religious belief" (377). Yet many would not consider Hope a modern poet at all. His isolation in Australia, his rejection of symbolism in favor of a discursive mode, and his use of traditional forms of versification all make him appear at odds with most of his contemporaries. Hope himself has written that he has "always by nature . . . been a more or less isolated individual not conscious of belonging in any real sense to a clan, a group, a class or even an organization" (*NComp,* 29).

Yet throughout his work one sees the ghosts of other poets, not merely Yeats and Auden in this century, but shades of the romantics, poets of the Enlightenment, and certainly the metaphysicals. Neil Corcoran echoes Dr. Johnson's indictment of the metaphysical poets when he writes that "Hope's great effort is to yoke himself—by as much violence as it takes—to 'literature' " (919). And David Kalstone has noted that it is "rare to find—as one does with Hope—poems that depend so

successfully on a shared sense of community" (621). The subject matter, the figures in his poems, the frequent use of myth (though the myths are often highly altered), reinforce the image of the poet firmly fixed in the community of tradition. One of his many concerns about free verse is how it separates the poet writing it from the tradition of the language in which he's writing.

But if Hope can be placed in a tradition that existed up to his time, can he also be placed among his contemporaries? Before I attempt an answer, it is perhaps appropriate to examine briefly the most obvious ways in which Hope diverges from the modernist tradition.

One element the romantics introduced to the English tradition was the idea of the individual, the poet as isolated from society because of his or her gift. Before that time, the poet was seen as a social being whose art served social ends or the gentleman who dabbled in verse on the side. But on closer analysis, one sees that this image of the isolated, alienated artist was most un-English and did not take hold until nearly the twentieth century, though it was a popular myth before that time. Wordsworth and Coleridge were both honored widely, Wordsworth the more so, but Coleridge had fame; that Coleridge was not so widely honored as Wordsworth had more to do with his output and personal life than it did with the larger society. The short, tragic lives of Shelley and Keats are romantic myths, but Shelley made a point of being as rebellious as possible and both died before they turned 30. Wordsworth was even more unknown than they at a comparable stage in his life. Blake had little fame, but he was an oddity, though a genius, an individual so unique that he seemed an enigma to his contemporaries.

The great popularizer of the misunderstood hero was Byron, who was, of the romantics, the most influenced by the eighteenth century and is the romantic poet with whom Hope shares most affinity. Though Byron outraged society, he was also tremendously popular, the best-selling poet until Tennyson. And with the mention of Tennyson, one need only think of the Victorians to see how honored, at least in title, the poets of the age were. The image of the mistreated poet doomed to obscurity and early death only became a partial reality in Germany, and even there, it tended to be as self-indulgent as it was destructive. The divorce of the poet from the larger society did not become a reality until the *fin de siecle* in England, and it was not until this century that the break was exacerbated to the point where today poets are kept by the universities much like wildlife on a preserve. And this state of affairs may largely be the fault of the poet.

Part of the root of the difficulty is a misreading of the romantic belief
in the primacy of the imagination, which is one place where Hope
diverges from most modernists. To begin with, Hope differentiates
between the imaginative faculties of the poet and his cousin, the novelist: "One shows the world as it is under the species of time, the other
creates the world as it might be under the species of eternity. 'The imagination,' said Keats, 'may be compared to Adam's dream—he woke and
found it truth.' It was the poet's imagination he meant. The novelist's
imagination on the other hand does not foreshadow the new Eve, but
interprets the old Adam to himself" (*NComp*, 37).

The primacy of the imagination, the visionary quality of depicting
the new Eve, locates the terrain of the poem in the landscape of the
vatic. And one sees just how far that theory has taken us today. A form
other than nonce is considered external to the organic nature of the
imagination and therefore inhibiting and unnatural to the workings of
the unconscious. A poem becomes a mysterious sounding of the depths
of the nonlogical aspects of the human mind. Its logic, if any exists, is
strictly internal. The private association is always preferred to the public
statement.

But is this the necessary end of such a theory of the imagination?
Certainly it wasn't for the romantics. Their poetry is accessible, as is
confirmed by its great popularity among poetry readers. Even the
dreamiest of romantic moods is objectified. Keats's nightingale is real,
the situation of the poem open to any attentive reader. But Keats's ode
brings up another interesting point. Hope notes that it is the cock, not
the hen, nightingale that sings, that he sings as often by day as by night,
and that the song is not one of ecstasy but is used to establish territory.
Certainly, these discrepancies do not seriously mar Keats's great poem—
Hope remarks that "Keats's superb ode is not touched; it depends on its
own truth." But he goes on to issue a warning: "we turn our back on the
other sort of truths at our peril—at the peril of the integrity of poetry.
They [truths of external reality] have their own beauty and they are not
hostile to the imagination. In the end they are necessary to it, if poetry is
not to lose touch with the real world" (*BA*, 34).

One understands Hope's concern with certain factual errors made by
Keats: any altering of physical reality is a move away from the actual.
Whereas a genius of Keats's abilities could write successfully and still
take a number of liberties, lack of attention to detail eventually shows
that the physical world is not properly honored. When too many liberties are taken, the outside world, anything beyond the poet's self, ceases

to matter at all. While the major poets have avoided this trap, many of their less fortunate peers have become bogged down in the swamp of self.

Hope is himself primarily a poet of the imagination rather than the observed world. In an essay, "Frost at Midday" (*Cave,* 101), he contrasts Wordsworth and Coleridge, Wordsworth as the poet of observable forms and Coleridge of the imagined, whose poetry was more influenced by his reading than by his walks. Hope clearly identifies in many aspects with Coleridge and often writes with highly imagined landscapes. But they are always grounded in the actual. Hope, echoing Sidney, wrote that the poet's "licence . . . is to create quite another nature than that in which he lives, though he must find his elements there" (*NComp,* 37).

The last cautionary note is essential. The reality surrounding the poet is the source of the poem. The mind, in both its conscious and unconscious aspects, transforms this material into art, brings its subjective element to play upon the objective world. And it is against this objective reality outside the poet that the poem must be tested. Otherwise, one is left with only subjective means to form aesthetic judgments, and Hope points out that the "view that poetry is primarily self-expression has been unfortunate in many ways." Such a theory of aesthetics implies that, "as it is the function of art to give expression to the artist's emotional life and vision, any means which satisfies him is a work of art. So to prefer one work of art to another is either meaningless . . . or else it is an attempt at *elitism.* . . . there is no objective criterion of judgement" (*NC,* 135). Art is an expression of the self, but it is that expression objectified. In a late poem, "On the Night Shift" (*O,* 17), Hope pictures the unconscious as night-shift workers who take over his brain while he sleeps. He remarks that he needs their help, but they need his help as well in his conscious translation of their raw material to achieved art: "Without me in their wild surreal play / Formless inconsequence would prove their curse."

A work of art is an objective thing; it may have been molded into shape in the furnace of the inner self but as it cools in the air it enters the world of objects and is from, but no longer of, the artist. It is offered up to the world of objects that provided its original impetus; it enters into a conversation with that which is outside the artist: "The proper role of poetry is, of course, to be what it is, to follow the inner law of its involvement of the imagination with the actual. . . . its obligation is to take its place in what Michael Oakeshott has splendidly described as the 'Conversation of Mankind' " (*NC,* 172).

One needs to look much earlier in the *Cratylus* to find exactly what is meant here by conversation. Self-expression is, of course, a part of conversation, but only a part. Conversation, as Hope uses it in this context, is also more than communication, as we most commonly use the word, "though it is based on two-way communication. The parties to a conversation are not necessarily exchanging information, though a good deal of information may in fact be exchanged. What they are primarily engaged in exchanging is awareness of each other's minds." He describes the mode of conversation as being "contemplation, discovery and recognition" and then brings the analogy home to poetry: "There is a sense in which a poem is a kind of conversation with an unknown person, with a mind which is imagined and projected into space by the poem itself, like the pollen grains of wind-inseminated plants scattered out to find their opposite numbers" (*NC,* 19). A poem, for Hope, takes as its raw material the world outside the poet; it is shaped within and offered again to the world without. The "conversation with an unknown person" means the exchange of consciousness goes both ways. In most ages, such a definition would be so much a basic assumption that it would not need stating. It does however go against the grain of modernism.

Hope stresses that this "conversation" demands clarity. Too often clarity is confused with simplification. What is clear can often be complex, but its complexity exists because of its faithfulness to a complex reality. Complexity in itself should not be the goal. Many of the favorite practices of modernism sacrifice clarity for the sake of an excessive allusiveness. It is true that the reader can be expected to supply something and should not be ignorant of tradition. It is also true that we can no longer assume that every educated person possesses a solid classical grounding. But poetry that is overly allusive tends to become too private; though the material may be taken from the public realm, it is either too arcane or too various to communicate to anyone but scholars. If allusion becomes the main substance of the poem, if allusion connected to allusion provides the movement of the work, then the reader is at as much a loss as if the poet had grafted together entirely personal happenings from his or her own life. The conversation breaks down, to be replaced by an intellectual pastiche; the canvas becomes a jumbled collage. Large sections of Pound's *Cantos,* for example, fall into this trap.

Another consideration is the modern poet's use of symbols. Hope's work is certainly full of symbols, but he by no means could be considered a symbolist poet. As Leonie Kramer points out, when Hope attempts the transcendent in his verse, he uses "the mode of the discur-

sive poet, not the oblique and tangential style of the symbolist" (32). At the very moment when many poets become most unclear, Hope is lucid. His efforts in this manner are not always successful, but at least readers know they are not.

Hope expressed his concerns on the excesses of symbolism in this passage on Baudelaire and Mallarme: "Where Baudelaire, however mysterious, is always definite and crystal clear, Mallarme turned poetry into a sort of puzzle game in which the subject was never referred to or described directly but, as he thought, more effectively evoked by allusion and hint. He may be said to have led a whole generation of poets into a wasteland of rather pointless obscurity" (*BA*, 73). Although Hope readily acknowledges Mallarme's genius, he finds that his influence has been disastrous for poets who followed him and led others "into a wasteland." Hope certainly ranks Eliot foremost in this group, granting that while Eliot was "quite good at light verse . . . his attempts at serious poetry are for the most part pretentious failures in a dispirited and flabby sort of free verse that was doomed from the start" (*BA*, 87).

Hope thus comes down on the side of clarity against allusiveness, and I think his own poetry bears him out on this. In few cases are the poems lacking within them the key to unlock their secrets. The obscurities of a poem such as "Morning Coffee" are certainly not the rule with Hope. Yet his poetry is neither simple nor does it shy away from difficult subject matter. However, Hope often seems torn between the poet's vatic and civic roles. His Orphic claims for poetry do not always mesh well with his stated preference for the civic mode of discourse. His Holofernes, Sackville, and Vivaldi poems seem a bit pedestrian in their delivery of large themes. A work such as "Flower Poem" (*CP*, 14) elicits more of the Orphic element of poetry in a stronger, even demonic mode. In the poem, the speaker rejects the posed flowers in a vase for something more elemental: "Between their legs the hairy flowers in bloom / Thrill at the amorous comparison." Hope affirms the life-enhancing nature of poetry, that only poetry can protect them "bleeding from their civilization."

The work of art is not a "cut flower but the entire plant" that is "Rooted in dung, dirt, dead men's bones." But he goes on to state that the aroma and beauty of the flower are "not in themselves the end." The end is found in the "ache of the mysterious event." Hope traces this back along the root to the lode of myth where the "subterranean river roars" and in the company of the troll and his knife, "the grinning girls / Sit spinning the bright fibre of their sex." Whatever its faults, "Flower

Poem" seems to come closer to that mysterious realm of the creative than do Hope's more discursive attempts. Yet even with the emotion, if not violence, inherent in "Flower Poem," it provides a clear entrance and is a consciously crafted object.

With an interest in clarity comes an intense awareness of craft. The poem as a well-made thing is crucial to his aesthetic; the poet as craftsperson is central to Hope's vision of the conscious artist: "Although I have spent most of my life in teaching and academic work, I am pleased that my background and connexions are with [the] world of country towns, small businesses and skilled trades and, as a poet, I like to think that I share and continue a tradition of craftsmanship" (*NComp,* 30). "Craftsmanship" is a key word, not only because of craft, but because through craft the poet is united with other human beings. Hope not only rejects the narcissistic element in much modern and most postmodern verse, he also continually attempts to tie himself to the tradition of Western literature and, through this tradition, to the great adventure of humankind.

This need for identification of the self with the other through the medium of craft is stressed in his essay "The Discursive Mode" (*Cave,* 1) when he claims, against most modern practice, that "poets have no need . . . of theories of magic or techniques of chance collision or subterranean evocation." Rather, Hope asserts, "poetry is simple"; he then goes on to define his conception of poetry as the "natural use of natural forms to produce effects never known in nature and to make these forces serve ends, not different from those met with in other kinds of social intercourse, but only at a heightened level of perception and a higher organization of heart and mind. And it is in this use of natural forces to new ends that poetry takes its place among the characteristically human and humane occupations" (*Cave,* 7).

Modern poetry has thirsted after novelty; the urge to make it new has resulted in such a proliferation of schools of verse that the literary landscape is strewn with the many *-isms* of this century. Whereas in the past when a maverick seemingly broke from the tradition and thereby enriched that very tradition, that poet remained a maverick, most poets today look at difference as a way of establishing a voice. The interesting thing about most talented mavericks of the past, the Blakes, the Hopkinses, and so forth, is that they cannot be copied extensively—they cannot propagate a school because all but the most subtle adaptations of their idiosyncrasies make their followers seem mere imitators. Most major poets of any period resemble each other in at least superficial

ways. Our age has courted oddity and attempted to mint it. What worked, if indeed it worked, for Eliot or Williams or Olson cannot be followed with slavishness because the territory staked out is too narrow; they are oddities, the proverbial exceptions that prove the rule. To follow in their tracks is to reach a dead end.

Hope affirms his allegiance to tradition and his distance from the modernists several times throughout his writing and indicates time after time that modernism's great mistake was to attempt to break itself off from tradition. He remarks that "poetry is no longer an integral part of daily life" and puts the onus for most of the blame on the poets themselves:

> Poetry in the past fifty years or so has largely become a private and even a secretive affair; its language has tended to become increasingly complicated and obscure, as though to repel the vulgar crowd and protect the interests of the initiates. If society on the whole ignores them, they have, on the whole, retorted by cutting themselves off from society. Under pretext of being *avant-garde* and experimental, of enlarging the bounds of their art, they become more and more esoteric, cranky, and erratic. They move further and further out into the unreal. (149)

Hope goes on to compare two passages, one a section of Tennyson's "In Memoriam" and the other one of John Berryman's "Dream Songs." Both deal with personal loss and are centered around Christmas. Hope shows how, though both poems are filled with personal associations, the Tennyson poem "speaks in a public language accessible to all readers of his day"; the Berryman poem, on the other hand, Hope finds to be an example of "wilful solipsism," a poetry produced by someone with a "sense of indulging in an abnormal, or even an unreal, activity in producing it" (*NC*, 151–52).

Hope then notes that in "present day America and in much of the world beside, the poet feels no obligation to his reader. He believes either that he is a sort of dark oracle or that he has no contract to communicate." Such work will attract small groups of the devout who value their distance from the society at large in a manner similar to that of street gangs, but "the rest of the world treats their poetry as a trivial game." Hope comments that he finds the contemporary situation especially "depressing because poets of great talent are rare enough and it is sad to see a man of real and exciting talent like Berryman, as his earlier poems revealed him to be, lost in such a blind labyrinth" (*NC*, 152).

So where does Hope fit? It is clear, from his craft and his concerns, that his work is a natural progression in the tradition of poetry in English; one can read the poets of the nineteenth century and easily imagine Hope's poetry following consistently enough from it, though he is by no means a predictable poet. The difficulty is, of course, that he is writing in an age that doesn't see natural progression as a virtue.

However, Hope poses an even greater quandary because of his linguistic abilities. I have considered Hope in the tradition of poetry only in English largely because of my linguistic limitations, limitations Hope does not share. In "Western Elegies V: The Tongues" (*O,* 11), Hope remarks that the "man who has only one tongue lives forever alone on an island / Shut in on himself by conventions he is only dimly aware of." He then mentions his readings in Latin, Italian, French, Spanish, Portuguese, Icelandic, German, Old Norse, Anglo-Saxon, and Russian. He can also read Greek and Arabic. The writers in these languages have had significant impact on Hope's writing and aesthetics. Certainly Kevin Hart is correct when he writes that the "hard work of interpreting Hope *sub specie* comp. lit. has yet to be done. . . . Very few Australian critics, if any, are sufficiently confident in foreign languages to begin that labour of comparison" (58).

But where does he fit in with his English language contemporaries? To place Hope properly, one has to create a counterview to the modernist pantheon that seems at times carved in stone. Judging one's own period is always guesswork. One is too close to, too involved with, the subject and has one's own vested interests at heart. But the most reliable way has always been from an overview, not just looking at the century in question from its own terms, but in looking at this time as part of the tradition from whence it sprang. If this is to remain the case, we are in for a healthy reevaluation of just what constitutes the important verse of our time.

Our age is in many ways a time of theory rather than great poetry. As our poetry whimpers out in its postmodern meandering so prominently displayed in such forums as the *American Poetry Review,* the theorists seem more in place than ever. But many periods are actually losing their energy just when they appear most energetic. They become overly ornate like the Rococo. Certainly, theory has never been as ornate as it appears now in our various poststructuralisms. And there are hopeful signs of a return to reason; Timothy's Steele's *Missing Measures* and Dana Gioia's essays are particularly promising.

Be that as it may, poetry will be redeemed ultimately only by poetry itself and the infusion of good sense; though good poets do not always

make good critics, the creation of quality poetry would once again make criticism literature's handmaiden rather than its guide. The very term modernism is problematic. It is evidence of a critical solipsism and has produced the absurdity of our now being considered postmodernists. Something is modern if it is contemporary; only an age dominated by critical theory and a sense of discontinuity rather than by art would ever have tolerated such a tag in the first place.

Certainly Yeats is a great poet for the ages, though he did talk much nonsense. I also believe that Auden will come to seem perhaps the central poet of English in this century. As with any poet who wrote prolifically, his work needs substantial winnowing, and the poetry of his last decade or so, while frequently charming, generally lacks greatness. His reputation cannot be hurt by having a superb literary executor, Edward Mendelson. Frost is an important poet, and some of Robinson will last. When considering other fine, more contemporary poets such as Richard Wilbur, Philip Larkin, and Seamus Heaney, one senses Hope's name might not be out of place here. His reputation seems even more hopeful when considering the younger poets often working in traditional forms who have emerged in the 1980s; of those prominent in this group, Dana Gioia and R. S. Gwynn have both written favorably of Hope.

If this summary seems somewhat arbitrary, I must plead guilty, but I think that a future view will attempt to restore continuity and not treat discontinuity as a virtue. If so, Hope should do very well indeed. Regardless, most poets survive today in anthologies, and Hope has a number of poems that should lend themselves to such collections. His appears a particularly hopeful situation because of the state of the language today. As English becomes more and more an international language, it becomes less and less possible to consider individual poetries in English, which are separated by artificial boundaries, as complete in themselves. Australia and other postcolonial literatures might no longer be ghettoized, and Hope is the major representative of Australian verse. If Australia is included, Hope must be as well; no other Australian poet, including Les Murray, has such breadth and depth of concern. Paul Kane has written that "No reader of Australian poetry, from a distance, can fail to see how major a figure Hope is on the landscape—for a long time, in fact, he was mistaken for the horizon itself."[1]

Regardless of the shifting winds of critical fashion, Hope's work remains substantial. Despite his conflicting approaches to the world, his use of various dualities posed and re-posed to offer fresh variations, he has from the beginning displayed a remarkable consistency in his con-

cern for form. It places him within the tradition of verse in English simultaneously as it distances him from many of his contemporaries, but in this he has never wavered.

Daniel Hoffman pointed out that "Hope's devotion to rhymed iambic pentameter is . . . the necessary expression of his convictions about the world."[2] Though he published his first book at the age of 48, his belief in poetry and its relation to the external world go back a good time before that. Hope notes that it was at about the age of 10 that he "conceived the idea of a poet as a man looking out from the place inside where thinking and feeling goes on and celebrating what he sees. From that time on I knew where I was going" (NC, 12).

Notes and References

Introduction

1. A. D. Hope, *Native Companions: Essays and Comments on Australian Literature 1936–1966* (Sydney: Angus & Robertson, 1974), 8; hereafter cited in text as *NC*.

2. A. D. Hope, *Chance Encounters* (Melbourne: Melbourne University Press, 1992), 41; hereafter cited in text as *CE*.

3. Cecil Hardgraft, *Australian Literature: A Critical Account to 1955* (London: Heinemann, 1962), 198; hereafter cited in text.

Chapter One

1. Rex Ingamells, "Environmental Values," in *Conditional Culture. The Oxford Anthology of Australian Literature,* eds. Leonie Kramer and Adrian Mitchell (Melbourne: Oxford University Press, 1985), 199–201; hereafter cited in text.

2. James McAuley, "The Grinning Mirror," in *The Oxford Anthology of Australian Literature,* eds. Leonie Kramer and Adrian Mitchell (Melbourne: Oxford University Press, 1985), 212–16; hereafter cited in text.

3. Eve Langley, "Australia," in *The Oxford Anthology of Australian Literature,* eds. Leonie Kramer and Adrian Mitchell (Melbourne: Oxford University Press, 1985), 251; hereafter cited in text.

4. R. A. Simpson, "Landscape," in *The Oxford Anthology of Australian Literature,* eds. Leonie Kramer and Adrian Mitchell (Melbourne: Oxford University Press, 1985), 418; hereafter cited in text.

5. Kenneth Slessor, "South Country," in *A Map of Australian Verse,* ed. James McAuley (Melbourne: Oxford University Press, 1975), 189; hereafter cited in text.

6. James McAuley, "Envoi," in *The Oxford Anthology of Australian Literature,* eds. Leonie Kramer and Adrian Mitchell (Melbourne: Oxford University Press, 1985), 216; hereafter cited in text.

7. James McAuley, *Under Aldebaran* (Melbourne: Melbourne University Press, 1946) 51; hereafter cited in text.

8. Judith Wright, *Preoccupations in Australian Poetry* (Melbourne: Oxford University Press, 1966), 31; hereafter cited in text.

9. Judith Wright, *The Double Tree* (Boston: Houghton Mifflin, 1978), 65; hereafter cited in text.

10. Harry Heseltine, "Australian Image: The Literary Heritage," in *The Oxford Anthology of Australian Literature,* eds. Leonie Kramer and Adrian

Mitchell (Melbourne: Oxford University Press, 1985), 298–312; hereafter cited in text.

11. Alec King, "Contemporary Australian Poetry," in *The Oxford Anthology of Australian Literature,* eds. Leonie Kramer and Adrian Mitchell (Melbourne: Oxford University Press, 1985), 444–51; hereafter cited in text.

12. Kenneth Slessor, "Five Visions of Captain Cook," in *A Book of Australian Verse,* ed. Judith Wright (Melbourne: Oxford University Press, 1962), 88; hereafter cited in text.

13. A. D. Hope, *Australian Literature 1950–1962* (Melbourne: Melbourne University Press, 1963), 6; hereafter cited in text as *Aus Lit.*

14. Leonie Kramer, *A. D. Hope* in Australian Writers and Their Work Series, ed. Grahame Johnston (Melbourne: Oxford University Press, 1979), 3; hereafter cited in text.

15. A. D. Hope, *The New Cratylus* (Melbourne: Oxford University Press, 1979), 91; hereafter cited in text as *NCrat.*

16. William Walsh, *A Manifold Voice: Studies in Commonwealth Literature* (London: Chatto & Windus, 1970), 135; hereafter cited in text.

17. Ken Goodwin, *A History of Australian Literature* (New York: St. Martin's, 1986), 217; hereafter cited in text.

18. Peter Kuch and Paul Kavanagh, "Daytime Thoughts about the Night Shift," interview with A. D. Hope, *Southerly,* no. 2 (1986): 221–31; hereafter cited in text.

19. A. D. Hope, *Collected Poems 1930–1965* (New York: Viking, 1976), 30–31; hereafter cited in text as *CP.*

20. Ross Mezger, "Alienation and Prophecy: The Grotesque in the Poetry of A. D. Hope," *Southerly* 36.3 (1976): 268–83; hereafter cited in text.

21. A. D. Hope, *Antechinus* (Sydney: Angus & Robertson, 1981), 21; hereafter cited in text as *Ant.*

Chapter Two

1. A. D. Hope, *The Cave and the Spring* (Chicago: University of Chicago Press, 1970), 68; hereafter cited in text as *Cave.*

2. Vivian Smith, "Poetry," in *The Oxford History of Australian Literature,* ed. Leonie Kramer (Melbourne: Oxford University Press, 1981), 372; hereafter cited in text.

3. Kevin Hart, *A. D. Hope* (Melbourne: Oxford University Press, 1992), 105; hereafter cited in text.

4. A. D. Hope, *Dunciad Minor: An Heroik Poem* (Carlton: Melbourne University Press, 1970), 22; hereafter cited in text as *Dunc.*

5. Gustav Cross, "The Poetry of A. D. Hope," in *The Literature of Australia,* ed. Geoffrey Dutton (Middlesex, England: Penguin, 1964), 383; hereafter cited in text.

6. Vincent Buckley, *Essays in Poetry: Mainly Australian* (Melbourne: Melbourne University Press, 1957), 150; hereafter cited in text.

Chapter Three

1. Neil Corcoran, review of *Selected Poems,* by A. D. Hope, *Times Literary Supplement* (22 August 1986): 919; hereafter cited in text.

2. A. D. Hope, *A Late Picking: Poems 1965–1974* (Sydney: Angus & Robertson, 1975), 45; hereafter cited in text as *LP.*

3. "Un-Australian Activities: Review of *New Poems 1965–1969,* by A. D. Hope," *Times Literary Supplement* (23 July 1970): 832; hereafter cited in text.

4. A. D. Hope, *New Poems 1965–1969* (New York: Viking, 1970), 9; hereafter cited in text as *NP.*

5. A. D. Hope, *A Midsummer Eve's Dream: Variations on a Theme by William Dunbar* (New York: Viking, 1970), 260–61; hereafter cited in text as *Eve.*

6. A. D. Hope, *Orpheus* (North Ryde: Angus & Robertson, 1991), 26; hereafter cited in text as *O.*

7. A. D. Hope *The Age of Reason* (Melbourne: Melbourne University Press, 1985), 115; hereafter cited in text as *AOR.*

8. Claude Rawson, review of *Selected Poems,* A. D. Hope, *Times Literary Supplement,* (24 July 1987): 783–84; hereafter cited in text.

9. Chris Wallace-Crabbe, "Three Faces of Hope," *Meanjin* 26.4 (1967): 407; hereafter cited in text.

10. William Jay Smith, review of *New Poems 1965–1969,* by A. D. Hope, *American Scholar* (Winter 1970): 174–78; hereafter cited in text.

Chapter Four

1. William Hazlitt, "Characters in Shakespeare's Plays: Coriolanus," *The Complete Works of William Hazlitt,* vol. 4, ed. P. P. How (London: J. M. Dent, 1930), 214–15; hereafter cited in text.

2. Christopher Marlowe, *The Tragical History of Doctor Faustus. Purged and Amended by A. D. Hope* (Canberra: Australian National University Press, 1982), 34; hereafter cited in text as *Faust.*

3. G. A. Wilkes and J. C. Reid, *The Literatures of Australia and New Zealand* (University Park: Pennsylvania State University Press, 1969), 142; hereafter cited in text.

Chapter Five

1. David Kalstone, "Two Poets," *Partisan Review* (Fall 1967): 619–25; hereafter cited in text.

2. David Kirby, review of *A Late Picking,* by A. D. Hope, *Times Literary Supplement* (7 April 1978): 394; hereafter cited in text.

Chapter Six

1. A. D. Hope, "Day-Time and Night-Time Vision," in *Australian Voices: Poetry and Prose of the 1970s,* ed. Rosemary Dobson (Canberra: Australian National University Press, 1975), 181; hereafter cited in text as "Day."
2. A. D. Hope, *A Book of Answers* (Sydney: Angus & Robertson, 1978), 34; hereafter cited in text as *BA.*

Chapter Seven

1. Ruth Morse, ed., *A. D. Hope. Selected Poems* (Manchester: Carcanet, 1986), 108; hereafter cited in text as *SP.*
2. R. F. Brissenden, review of *New Poems,* by A. D. Hope, *Southerly,* 30.2 (1970): 90; hereafter cited in text.
3. Geoffrey H. Hartmann, "Beyond the Middle Style," *Kenyan Review,* 25.4 (1963): 756; hereafter cited in text.

Conclusion

1. Paul Kane, review of *The Age of Reason,* by A. D. Hope, *Antipodes* 1, no. 1 (March 1987): 46; hereafter cited in text.
2. Daniel Hoffman, review of *New Poems* and *The Cave and the Spring,* by A. D. Hope, *New York Times Book Review,* Pt. 1 (21 February 1971), 28; hereafter cited in text.

Selected Bibliography

PRIMARY SOURCES

Books of Poetry

The Age of Reason. Melbourne: Melbourne University Press, 1985.
Antechinus. Sydney: Angus & Robertson, 1981.
A Book of Answers. Sydney: Angus & Robertson, 1978.
Collected Poems: 1930–1965. New York: Viking, 1966.
Collected Poems: 1930–1970. Sydney: Angus & Robertson, 1972.
Dunciad Minor: An Heroick Poem. Melbourne: Melbourne University Press, 1970.
A Late Picking: Poems 1965–1974. Sydney: Angus & Robertson, 1974.
New Poems: 1965–1969. Sydney: Angus & Robertson, 1969; New York: Viking, 1970.
Orpheus. Sydney: Angus & Robertson, 1991.
Poems. London: Hamish Hamilton, 1960; New York: Viking, 1960.
Selected Poems. Manchester: Carcanet, 1986.

Plays

Ladies from the Sea. Melbourne: Melbourne University Press, 1987.
The Tragical History of Doctor Faustus: By Christopher Marlowe, Purged and Amended by A. D. Hope. Canberra: Australian National University Press, 1982.

Books of Criticism

Australian Literature 1950–1962. Melbourne: Melbourne University Press, 1963.
The Cave and the Spring: Essays in Poetry. Chicago: University of Chicago Press, 1974.
Judith Wright. Melbourne: Oxford University Press, 1975.
A Midsummer Eve's Dream: Variations on a Theme by William Dunbar. New York: Viking, 1970.
Native Companions: Essays and Comments on Australian Literature 1936–1966. Sydney: Angus & Robertson, 1974.
The New Cratylus: Notes on the Craft of Poetry. Melbourne: Oxford University Press, 1979.
The Pack of Autolycus. Canberra: Australian National University Press, 1978.

The Structure of Verse and Prose. Sydney: Australasian Medical, 1963.

Memoirs

Chance Encounters. Melbourne: Melbourne University Press, 1992.

Interviews

A. D. Hope. Selected Poems. Interview by Ruth Morse. Tape recording, Broadbottom, Cheshire: Canto Carcanet, 1988.
"Daytime Thoughts about the Night Shift." Interview by Peter Kuch and Paul Kavanagh. *Southerly,* no. 2 (1986): 221–31.

SECONDARY SOURCES

Bibliographies

Hooton, Joy W. *A. D. Hope.* Melbourne: Oxford University Press, 1979. Helpful, but outdated, covering Hope's work only until 1979.

Selected Books, Parts of Books, and Articles

Brissenden, R. F. "Review of *New Poems,* by A. D. Hope." *Southerly* 30.2 (1970): 83–96. This is one of the fullest reviews of any individual volume of Hope's and a good general commentary on the poet's development as a poet to that point.
Buckley, Vincent. *Essays in Poetry: Mainly Australian.* Melbourne: Melbourne University Press, 1957. This is the first in-depth analysis of Hope's work, though limited, of course, to his early poetry. Buckley is especially insightful in his observations about the tactile nature of much of Hope's verse and Hope's claims to be a classical poet though much of his material is romantic.
Gwynn, R. S. "A. D. Hope." *Critical Survey of Poetry: Supplement.* Ed. Frank N. Magill. Englewood Heights: Salem, 1987, 184–92. An excellent overview of Hope's poetic career. Gwynn places particular emphasis on Hope's craftsmanship. The entry is interesting and one of the few articles on Hope written by an American poet in recent years.
Hart, Kevin. *A. D. Hope.* Melbourne: Oxford University Press, 1992. Part of the Australian Writers series, this book is a good overview of Hope's career. It generally avoids poststructural jargon, unlike some other books in the series, and stresses the Orphic nature of much of Hope's work.
Heseltine, Harry. "Australian Image: The Literary Heritage." In *Oxford Anthology of Australian Literature.* Eds. Leonie Kramer and Adrian Mitchell. Melbourne: Oxford University Press, 1985, 298–312. Heseltine is particularly good in his discussion of the element of horror and cruelty in

Australian literature. Though the essay is not solely about Hope, I found the entire article invaluable in approaching Hope's earlier poetry and seeing its Australian roots, which are not always easily discernible.

Kramer, Leonie. *A. D. Hope.* Melbourne: Oxford University Press, 1979. Part of the Australian Writers and Their Work series, this is generally a good overview of Hope's work until 1979. It is in many ways, however, superseded by Hart's book, as Hope's discursive and narrative poems of the 1980s allow one to see his opus in a more unified manner.

McAuley, James. *A Map of Australian Verse.* Melbourne: Oxford University Press, 1975. This is the best analysis of the dualities of Hope's earlier work. McAuley divides the verse into three basic groupings, the Apollonian, the Dionysian, and the Orphic. His recognition of the Orphic thus anticipates Kevin Hart's.

Wallace-Crabbe, Chris. "Three Faces of Hope." *Meanjin,* 26.4 (1967): 396–407). This piece stresses the dualistic nature of Hope's poetry to midcareer. Wallace-Crabbe comments that Hope is capable of lucid heights because the murky depths are so well explored. He also stresses the operatic nature of many of Hope's monologues and is particularly good in his discussion of the unexpected ending of Hope's tribute to Yeats.

Walsh, William. *A Manifold Voice: Studies in Commonwealth Literature.* London: Chatto & Windus, 1970. Walsh offers a good general survey of Hope through midcareer, putting the poet in a context of international literatures in English.

Index

The Author

Robert Darling is an associate professor of English at Keuka College in the Finger Lakes section of New York and did his doctoral work at the University of Rhode Island. He has published poetry in more than 50 periodicals in the United States, Canada, England, and Australia. The recipient of several awards for his poetry, Darling has given numerous readings. His critical writing has included chapters in reference works on contemporary poets and reviews on Australian poets in *Antipodes,* the journal of the American Association of Australian Literary Studies. Before joining academe, he worked in advertising, journalism, radio, and dispute mediation.

The Editor

Kinley E. Roby is professor emeritus of English at Northeastern University. He is the twentieth-century field editor of Twayne's English Authors Series, series editor of Twayne's Critical History of British Drama, and general editor of Twayne's Women and Literature Series. He has written books on Arnold Bennett, Edward VII, and Joyce Cary, and edited a collection of essays on T. S. Eliot. He makes his home in Naples, Florida.